BASIC JUDAISM FOR YOUNG PEOPLE: **ISRAEL**

BASIC JUDAISM
FOR YOUNG PEOPLE

VOLUME ONE

ISRAEL

NAOMI PASACHOFF, PH.D.

BEHRMAN HOUSE, INC., PUBLISHERS

WEST ORANGE, NEW JERSEY

To my first and best teachers,
Anna Jacobson Schwartz and Isaac Schwartz

DESIGNER: Martin Lubin/Betty Binns Graphics
ARTISTS: Marlies Merk Najaka and Jody Wheeler
PROJECT EDITOR: Geoffrey Horn

The editor and publisher gratefully acknowledge the cooperation of
the following sources of photographs for this book:

American ORT Federation, 112; Eve Arnold/Magnum, 4; Bill Aron, 2, 27, 70–71, 122, 127; Art Resource, 22; Micha Bar-Am/Magnum, 134–35; Albert Ben-Zion/ Magnum, 48–49; Jerry Bergman/Black Star, 47; Ian Berry/Magnum, 54; Bettmann Archive, 76, 77, 120; Björn Bölstad/Photo Researchers, 86; René Burri/ Magnum, 12, 14, 55, 116; Gordon Cahan/Photo Researchers, 54; Cornell Capa/ Magnum, 35, 82; Thomas S. England/Photo Researchers, 55; Elliott Erwitt/ Magnum, 41; Leonard Freed/Magnum, 54, 118; Paul Fusco/Magnum, 36, 41, 130, 140; Louis Goldman/Photo Researchers, 55; Erich Hartmann/Magnum, 38; Hebrew Union College–Skirball Museum, 62 (both photos), 113 (both photos); Israel Consulate General, 142; Ronny Jaques/Photo Researchers, 90–91; Jewish Museum/Art Resource, 56; Paolo Koch/Photo Researchers, 78; Hiroji Kubota/ Magnum, 54; Magnum, 74, 110; Roger Malloch/Magnum, 106; Chris Maynard/ Magnum, 65; Richard Nowitz/Black Star, 93, 94; Mathias Oppersdorff/Photo Researchers, 55; Jay M. Pasachoff, 32–33; Porterfield/Chickering/Photo Researchers, 99; David Rubinger/Black Star, 52; David Rubinger/Time Magazine, 132; Scala/Art Resource, 128; Marilyn Silverstone/Magnum, 28; Robert Smith/ Black Star, 98; United Jewish Appeal, 66.

The editor and publisher also wish to thank Arthur Kurzweil for his
assistance in developing this project.

Library of Congress Cataloging-in-Publication Data
(Revised for vol. 1)

Pasachoff, Naomi E.
    Basic Judaism for young people.

      "Artists: Marlies Merk Najaka and Jody Wheeler"—v. 1, p. ;
      "Artists: Tony Chen and Jody Wheeler"—v. 2, p.
      Includes indexes.
      Contents: v. 1. Israel—v. 2. Torah.
      1. Judaism—Juvenile literature. 2. Judaism—Dictionaries. I. Najaka,
Marlies, ill. II. Wheeler, Jody, ill. III. Chen, Tony, ill. IV. Title.
BM573.P37   1986   296   86-1214
ISBN 0-87441-423-7 (v. 1)

CONTENTS

FOREWORD:
TO THE TEACHER

The alphabetically arranged table of contents of our book, ranging from Adam and Bet Knesset to Tzionut and Tefutzot, shows just how broad the term "Israel" can be. It includes theology, ritual practice, love of land, and a host of values some regard as simply secular. Some students may be tempted to see Judaism as analogous to Christianity, with the synagogue as a sort of Jewish church, the rabbi as a counterpart to the priest. While similarities abound, the teacher must point to the unique character of Judaism, in its universalism and its particularism.

Both the universality and particularity of Jewish sacred culture are illustrated in this first of Naomi Pasachoff's more than basic books of Judaism for young people. The book begins with Adam, the father of humanity. The Bible itself, written for the Jewish people, does not begin with Abraham, the first Jew, but with Adam and Eve, the first human beings. Genesis shapes the character of Jewish universalism. The God of Israel is the God of humanity. However much the Bible focuses on the promise and fulfillment of the career of Israel, the God worshiped is never merely a tribal deity indifferent to other nations.

In their liturgical formula, the rabbis of Talmudic times insisted on referring to God as ‏מֶלֶךְ הָעוֹלָם‎,, the King of the universe. Thus Abraham, who is called to be a blessing to "all the families of the earth," argues with God to spare the righteous among the citizens of Sodom and Gomorrah. He is concerned *as a Jew* to defend the *non-Jewish* innocent. His appeal to God is from God, Whom he knows as ‏שֹׁפֵט כָּל־הָאָרֶץ‎, the Judge of all the earth. Abraham, the Jew, knows his task to be the defense of כְּבוֹד הַבְּרִיוֹת, the dignity of his fellow creatures. The dialogue between God and Abraham before Sodom is thus no incidental episode.

The rabbinic choice of reading the entire Book of Jonah on the sacred day of Yom Kippur is similarly laden with meaning. The rabbis wanted to chastise the parochialism of the prophet for "suppressing his prophecy." Jonah ben Amitai improperly seeks to restrict his prophetic gifts to his own people. He is taught that God's concern, and thus his own, may not exclude the people of Nineveh, who are not Jews.

Such examples of Jewish universalism are frequently challenged by Jewish thinkers who fear that the Jewish vineyard will not be tended because of the attention paid to humanitarian interests. These critics are sometimes right: a false universalism may indeed deflect attention from concern for Jewish interests. (George Santayana once spoke of pseudo-universalists who love humanity "in general," much in the manner of those who would speak "in general," without using any particular language.) To avoid this pitfall, the rabbis sought to balance the values of Jewish particularism with a distinctively Jewish universalism. For the sake of peace and the mending of a broken world, they prescribed a Jewish way: "Jews are obligated to support the poor of the Gentiles together with the poor of the Jews; to comfort their bereaved with tears; to bury their deceased as we bury our own" (T. Gittin). The rabbis observed that the Torah repeats the phrase "to love the stranger in thy midst" no fewer than eighteen times. They pointed to the tradition wherein Jews on Sukkot brought seventy bullocks to be sacrificed out of concern for the seventy nations of the world.

Adam and Abraham are both part of our tradition. So Jews are doubly covenanted. The Covenant of Noah makes us part of all humanity, whose responsibilities we share (Genesis 8). The Covenant of Abraham gives us the special responsibilities we assume with love in order to become a "blessing to all the families of the earth" (Genesis 12:2– 3).

Ben Azzai, a contemporary of Akiba, insisted that the essence of Judaism is grounded in these Biblical verses: "This is the book of the generations of Adam. In the day that God created man, in the likeness of God made He him; male and female created He them, and blessed them, and called their name Adam, in the day they were created" (Genesis 5:1– 2). Such is the inclusive and humanitarian spirit our *Israel* volume embodies.

RABBI HAROLD M. SCHULWEIS

PREFACE:
TO THE STUDENT

The word "Israel" should suggest many things to you. Many people use "Israel" to refer to the State of Israel, where any Jew may be a citizen and where Jewishness is part of everyone's daily life. "Israel" also means the land of Israel, and the word has often been applied as a name for the Jewish people. In addition, when "Israel" is used as a word for community, it describes our responsibilities toward one another. You will learn about all these meanings — and others — as you read this *Israel* volume.

Originally the word "Israel" meant "struggling with God." It comes from the famous Torah portion in which our ancestor Jacob struggled through the night with the "person of God" and somehow survived the ordeal.

This, too, is a proper meaning for the word, because Jews are always struggling. We struggle not only to be modern, but also to keep our traditions. We struggle not only to defend ourselves against our enemies, but also to hold on to our ideals of peace. We struggle not only to help those less fortunate than we are, but also to let them keep their sense of dignity and beauty.

We hope you find being Jewish an exciting challenge, and we hope you enjoy reading about the importance of Israel in the world. As you read this book, you may find the word "Israel" meaning different things to you at different times. You may have to struggle to define what Israel means to you. We hope you enjoy that struggle. We know that, like Jacob, you can win.

RABBI WILLIAM CUTTER

The Alef-Bet אָלֶף בֵּית

ENGLISH SOUND	ENGLISH NAME	NUMBER VALUE	HEBREW NAME	LETTER
—	alef	1	אָלֶף	א
b	bet	2	בֵּית	בּ
v	vet		בֵית	ב
g	gimmel	3	גִמֶל	ג
d	dalet	4	דָלֶת	ד
h	hay	5	הֵא	ה
v	vav	6	וָו	ו
z	zayin	7	זַיִן	ז
ḥ	ḥet	8	חֵית	ח
t	tet	9	טֵית	ט
y	yod	10	יוד	י
k	kaf	20	כָּף	כּ
ḥ	chaf		כָף	כ
ḥ	final chaf		כָף סוֹפִית	ך
l	lamed	30	לָמֶד	ל
m	mem	40	מֵם	מ
m	final mem		מֵם סוֹפִית	ם
n	nun	50	נוּן	נ
n	final nun		נוּן סוֹפִית	ן
s	samech	60	סָמֶךְ	ס
—	ayin	70	עַיִן	ע
p	pay	80	פֵּא	פּ
f	fay		פֵא	פ
f	final fay		פֵא סוֹפִית	ף
ts, tz	tzadee	90	צָדִי	צ
ts, tz	final tzadee		צָדִי סוֹפִית	ץ
k	kof	100	קוּף	ק
r	resh	200	רֵיש	ר
sh	shin	300	שִׁין	שׁ
s	sin		שִׂין	שׂ
t	tav	400	תָו	ת
t	tav		תָו	ת

Note: The ḥ sound is variously represented in English as ch, h, ḥ, or kh (e.g., **Ch**anukah or **Ḥ**anukkah, **ch**allah or **ḥ**allah, hala**ch**ah or hala**kh**ah).

INTRODUCTION:
ISRAEL, THE ALEF-BET,
AND TRUTH

One of the first things you learned when you began your Jewish education was the alef-bet, the Hebrew alphabet. This was your start in reading Hebrew, the language of the State of Israel and of the Jews, who are sometimes called by the name "Israel."

The subject of this book is Israel, both the people and the country. In the pages that follow, different topics about Israel are arranged in their Hebrew alphabetical order. The topics deal with the land of Israel, the Jewish people, and the relations of Jews with one another and with all humanity.

If you write out the letters of the alef-bet from alef (א) to tav (ת) and include in their places the five final letters (chaf, mem, nun, fay, tzadee), there are twenty-seven letters in all. The middle letter, surrounded by thirteen others on each side, is mem (מ). The first, middle, and last letters together—alef, mem, tav—spell out the Hebrew word for "truth," Emet (אֱמֶת).

The rabbis taught the importance of Emet. "Whoever strays from Emet is like a person who worships an idol instead of the God of truth." The rabbis stressed that Jews must be truthful in their dealings not only with each other but with non-Jews as well. The Jewish people must deal honestly with all human beings.

This book opens with a chapter on Adam (אָדָם), the Hebrew word both for the first human being and for all humankind.

There is an old story that, when God was ready to create Adam, He consulted the angels. Two angels,

The rabbis taught that Jews must deal honestly with all human beings. In business, that means a good product at a fair price.

named Kindness and Righteousness, encouraged God to create Adam. They knew that human beings would perform kind deeds, like giving Tzedakah. But two other angels, named Truth — אֱמֶת — and Peace — שָׁלוֹם — advised God not to create Adam.

Emet said, "Human beings will lie."

Shalom said, "Human beings will fight with one another."

God agreed with Kindness and Righteousness, and He created Adam. Then He took the angel named Emet and threw him to the earth.

The other angels were shocked. Why was God insulting Truth in this way? But God assured the angels that His reason for throwing Truth to the earth was to plant it there. Just as no one knows where a seed has been planted until it sprouts, so Emet might lie hidden on earth for a while. But eventually human beings would harvest Emet and live by it.

As this book leads you through the Hebrew alphabet, you will learn about some of the ways Jews have tried to make Emet flourish on earth. Just as אֱמֶת has letters from the beginning, middle, and end of the alefbet, so truth must be the beginning, middle, and end for the Jewish people.

אָדָם

ADAM
ä • däm'

Adam is the name of the first human being. Because all human beings are descendants of Adam, people are called "children of Adam," בְּנֵי אָדָם.

The name Adam comes from the Hebrew word for earth, אֲדָמָה. In the Bible, God uses the dust of the earth to create Adam in His image.

We are all children of Adam.

CHAPTER ONE

The Torah starts with a discussion of all humankind before it moves on to the history of the ancient Hebrews. According to the Bible, Adam and Eve were the first people.

Whether we accept this story literally or not, the traditional Jewish lessons from the story of Adam are still important.

Each one of us has two pockets, said a famous rabbi. Each pocket contains a message. One message reminds us of our limits, and the other message reminds us of our greatness. The first message says, "I am earth and dust." If we are feeling too proud, we need to read that message. The other message says, "The world was created for my sake." Whenever we feel down in the dumps, that message should give us hope.

In this chapter, you will learn that people have a special dignity because they are created in God's image. You will also read why the Bible says God gave all of us one common ancestor.

CHAPTER SUMMARY

Lesson 1: We must treat others and ourselves as if we were images of God.

Lesson 2: Since all human beings have a common ancestor, all people are of equal worth.

We are created in God's image

The Torah teaches that God created Adam in His own image. Now, Jews do not believe that God has a body. So what does it mean to say that human beings are created in God's image? It means that we have some Godlike abilities. Only human beings can recognize God and try to bring Godliness into the world. Since all human beings are created in God's image, we must treat other

◀

One way we can be like God is to make full use of our creative powers.

people and ourselves in the same dignified way. As you read the two stories that follow, look for answers to these questions:

(a) How was Rabbi Elazar ben Simeon taught a lesson about treating others as images of God?

(b) How did Hillel teach his students to treat themselves as images of God?

TREATING OTHERS AS IMAGES OF GOD

Rabbi Elazar ben Simeon took such great pride in his learning that he began to look down on other people. One day, as he rode along on his donkey, the rabbi saw an ugly man with a twisted body. The man recognized the rabbi and greeted him.

"What a pleasure it is for me to meet the learned Rabbi Elazar ben Simeon," said the man. "I hope I find you in good health."

Rabbi Elazar did not return the greeting. Instead he asked, "Are all your townspeople as ugly as you?"

The man answered, "Take your complaint to my Maker."

Rabbi Elazar immediately understood that he had insulted not only the man but also God. The great scholar got down from his donkey and, bowing before the man he had insulted, begged forgiveness.

"Of what use is all my learning," said Rabbi Elazar, "if it has not taught me that you are created in God's image just as I am?"

TREAT YOURSELF AS AN IMAGE OF GOD

One day, the great teacher Hillel left class together with his students. As he turned to leave them, his students asked where he was going. "I am going to observe a Mitzvah now," said Hillel.

HAVE YOU HEARD?

Rabbi Akiba taught the same lesson Hillel did, but under much more difficult conditions. The Romans put Akiba in prison because he refused to stop teaching Torah. While he was in prison, the Romans gave him a small amount of water each day. Instead of using this water to quench his thirst, Akiba used it for washing. Like the other great rabbis, Akiba believed that "we must all wash our face, hands, and feet daily in honor of our Maker."

The students were surprised when they saw Hillel head for the bathhouse that was near the school. After all, they knew that Mitzvah (מִצְוָה) meant a religious commandment. "How is bathing a Mitzvah?" they asked.

Hillel pointed to a nearby statue. "Why is that statue kept so clean?" he asked.

"Because it is made in the king's image," answered the students. "To neglect it would show disrespect."

"Think how much more disrespectful it is to neglect to keep our own bodies clean," said Hillel. "After all, we are created in the image of the King of Kings — God Himself. So whenever we bathe, we do a Mitzvah."

REVIEW IT

1. What basic belief does the story about Rabbi Elazar ben Simeon share with the story about Hillel?

2. Think back to the story of the two pockets that you read at the beginning of this chapter. Which message should Rabbi Elazar have read before speaking to the ugly man? Which message might have helped Hillel's students understand why bathing is a Mitzvah?

Just as a statue is made in the image of a king, so we are made in God's image.

Adam: our common ancestor

The Torah says that when God created the world, He created different kinds of plants and animals. But when God made people, He began with only a single human being—Adam. After you read the following section, you should be able to answer this question:

What lessons can we learn from the idea that all human beings have a single ancestor?

ALL PEOPLE HAVE GREAT AND EQUAL VALUE

The rabbis thought of several ways to explain why God started with a single human being. The first is that we are all like Adam: each of us is worthy of having a world created for us.

The second is that each person is as important as all of humanity. Whoever kills a single human being can be thought of as destroying all humankind. Whoever helps keep a single person alive can be thought of as saving all humankind.

A third explanation points out that if God had started by creating more than one person, each person's descendants might then say, "Our ancestors were greater than your ancestors." But since all people have a common ancestor, no group can claim that it is better than any other.

REVIEW IT

1. Give three explanations for God's creating only a single Adam.

2. Which explanation do you prefer? Why would you choose it over the others?

HAVE YOU HEARD?

"The rabbis" is a common term for those Jewish scholars whose opinions we read in such ancient texts as the Mishnah, the Midrash, and the Talmud. In this book, the word "rabbi" is often used along with the name of a particular scholar. Some of these rabbis, such as Akiba and Tarfon, lived in ancient times. Others, like Levi Yitzḥak of Berditchev and Moshe Leib of Sassov, lived more recently in the Jewish communities of Europe. Still others are leading today's Jewish communities in Israel and in the Tefutzot. But when you see the phrase "the rabbis," the words always refer to the ancient scholars.

אֶרֶץ יִשְׂרָאֵל

ERETZ YISRAEL
e′rets yis • rä • āl′

Eretz Yisrael is the land of Israel. Jews have lived in Eretz Yisrael for more than 3000 years. Wherever Jews have lived throughout their history, they have always thought of Eretz Yisrael as a special homeland.

Rugged in landscape and rich in tradition, Eretz Yisrael holds a special place in the hearts of the Jewish people.

CHAPTER TWO

Over the entire history of the Jewish people, Eretz Yisrael has been a special place both for the Jews who lived there and for Jews who could only imagine it.

In this chapter, you will learn about the special feeling Jews have for Eretz Yisrael. You will also learn about a Jewish poet whose poems expressed great love for Eretz Yisrael. His love was shared by many other Jews who did not live there.

CHAPTER SUMMARY

Lesson 1: Jews have always had a special love for Eretz Yisrael.

Lesson 2: Yehudah HaLevi's love for Eretz Yisrael was as strong in his life as it was in his poetry.

God, Eretz Yisrael, and the Jews

According to an old legend, God said to Moses, "Eretz Yisrael pleases Me, and the people of Israel please Me. I shall bring the people who please Me into the land that pleases Me." As you read more about the relationship between God, Eretz Yisrael, and the people of Israel, ask yourself this question:

How does the story of Creation support the idea that Eretz Yisrael belongs to the Jewish people?

◄
Yehudah HaLevi was so thrilled to be in Jerusalem that he did not realize his life was in danger.

THE CREATION STORY AND ERETZ YISRAEL

Some Jews use the story of Creation to support their belief that Eretz Yisrael belongs to the Jewish people.

One rabbi asked, "Why does the Torah begin with the story of Creation? Why doesn't it start instead with the first Mitzvah that God commanded?" The rabbi an-

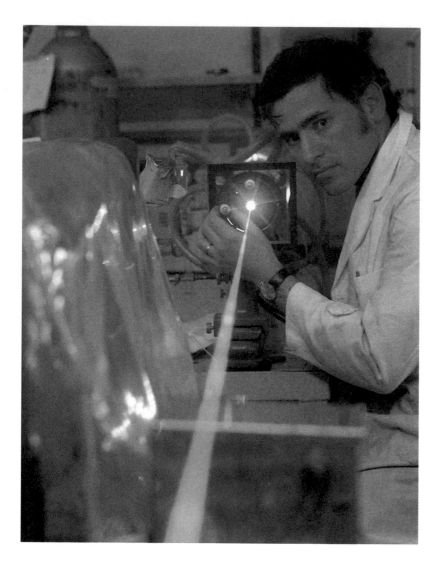

Today, scientists in Eretz Yisrael are using advanced technology to discover the wonders of God's Creation.

swered his own question by saying that the Torah begins with the story of Creation in order to strengthen the claim of the Jews to Eretz Yisrael.

He explained that the nations of the world might challenge the Jews' right to the land by saying, "You are a nation of thieves. The land you claim as your own you stole from the seven nations who lived there before you!"

Because the Torah describes how God created the whole world, the rabbi continued, the Jews have a ready answer to those who challenge them. They can say, "The entire world is God's. He created it, and it is His to do with it whatever He wants to. At first God gave the land to those seven nations willingly, but then He took it from them and gave it willingly to us."

Some people take a different view. They suggest that the Jews' claim to the land is based on the fact that Jews first lived in Eretz Yisrael as a distinct people. It is natural for Jews to identify themselves with their land, just as any people can have a special love for their homeland.

Throughout history there have been other explanations of the Jewish yearning for Eretz Yisrael. For example, whenever Jews have been oppressed outside of Eretz Yisrael, some people have felt strongly that only with a homeland would Jews be safe.

REVIEW IT

1. Give three explanations for the special love Jews have always felt for Eretz Yisrael.

2. What do these explanations have in common? How are they different from one another?

3. Which of these explanations is closest to your own feeling about Eretz Yisrael?

Yehudah HaLevi and the love of Eretz Yisrael

Over the centuries, many Jews who were unable to live in Eretz Yisrael continued to feel a strong love for it. Yehudah HaLevi was a great Hebrew poet who captured the longing that many Jews felt but were unable to ex-

If you look closely, you can see the Jerusalem skyline above the rolling hills of the Judean desert.

Writers of Jewish history use B.C.E. (Before the Common Era) to mean what Christian writers mean by B.C. (Before Christ). Similarly, Jews substitute the abbreviation C.E. (Common Era) for A.D. (Anno Domini, a Latin phrase meaning "In the year of our Lord"). In this way, Jews can make use of the regular calendar without accepting the Christian belief in Jesus as the "Christ," a word meaning "Messiah."

press for themselves. Read more about Yehudah HaLevi's love for Eretz Yisrael, and ask yourself:

What are two ways in which Yehudah HaLevi showed his love for Eretz Yisrael?

YEHUDAH HALEVI'S FINAL JOURNEY

Yehudah HaLevi was born in Spain around 1075. In addition to being a great poet, he was also a successful physician and a philosopher. His writings and his profession made him well known and well-to-do. Yet Yehudah HaLevi was not satisfied with his life.

The most important thing for him was his love of Eretz Yisrael. His poems sang of his deep longing for Eretz Yisrael.

After many years, Yehudah HaLevi decided to make the dangerous journey. His plan was to sail to Egypt and then to go overland to Eretz Yisrael. When he arrived in Egypt, he began to feel a new strength. After all, he was now in the country where God had performed many miracles for the Israelites. But the poet knew that he had not yet reached his goal.

WHAT TIME IS IT?

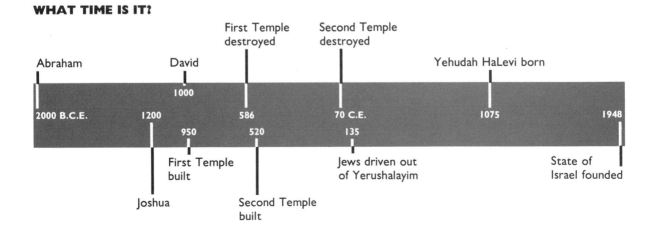

According to legend, when Yehudah HaLevi finally entered the city of Jerusalem, he remembered the words of one of the Psalms: "Her very stones are dear to God's servants." So Yehudah HaLevi removed his shoes to be able to touch the stones directly.

Then he began to recite from the most famous of his poems about Eretz Yisrael: "I will fall to my face on your earth and love your stones and dust."

As he did these things, Yehudah HaLevi was unaware that he was being watched by a man on horseback.

The horseman grew angrier and angrier as he saw how devoted this foreigner was to the land. Digging his feet into the sides of his horse, he forced the animal to trample Yehudah HaLevi and kill him.

Yehudah HaLevi's hopes of living in Eretz Yisrael died with him. But his poems did not die. Over the ages, they continued to express the love Jews felt for Eretz Yisrael even though they were unable to live there.

REVIEW IT

1. In what country did Yehudah HaLevi stop on his way to Eretz Yisrael?

2. Why did the poet feel special when he got to this country?

3. Describe a time when you knew you were close to some goal but had not yet achieved it. How did you feel?

בֵּית כְּנֶסֶת

BET KNESSET
bāt kə • nes'et

The Hebrew **Bet Knesset** means almost exactly the same as the Greek (and now English) word "synagogue." Both mean "meeting place." The Bet Knesset replaced the ancient Temple as the center of Jewish religious life.

The Bet Knesset is where Jews join together in prayer.

CHAPTER THREE

A rabbi once compared the relationship between a Jew and the Bet Knesset to the relationship between a branch and a tree. As long as it is still attached to the tree, even the weakest branch has a chance to grow strong again. But once the branch falls off the tree, there is no hope of its regaining strength.

In this chapter, you will learn when and why the Bet Knesset became such an important part of Jewish life. You will also learn some legends that explain why the Bet Knesset is considered a "little Temple."

CHAPTER SUMMARY

Lesson 1: After the destruction of the First Temple, the Bet Knesset became an important part of Jewish life.

Lesson 2: The Bet Knesset is like a "little Temple."

How the Bet Knesset came to be so important

Has anything ever happened to you that at first seemed too terrible for words but later turned out all right? In Jewish history, such events have taken place more than once. As you learn how the Bet Knesset became so important in Jewish life, ask yourself:

What disaster made the Bet Knesset so important?

BABYLONIA AND THE BET KNESSET

The ancient Hebrews used to worship God by making animal sacrifices. After King Solomon's Temple was built, people could bring their sacrifices only to the Temple in Jerusalem.

In 586 B.C.E., Jewish life was changed forever. Babylonian invaders destroyed the Temple and drove most of the Jews out of the land. These two events were the worst blow imaginable to the Jews. Without the Temple,

◄

In ancient Israel, people brought animals to the Temple as gifts for God. The sacrifices were conducted by priests, who had to be born into the priesthood.

they could not make sacrifices. In Babylonia, how could they continue to be Jews?

To discuss their common problems and to figure out how to worship God without a Temple, the Jews may have gathered on Shabbat, the day of rest that only Jews observed. They may have studied Torah to see how they had sinned and how they might prove to God that they were worthy to return to Eretz Yisrael. They may also have read the words of their prophets, who had warned that disaster would strike unless they changed their ways. For example, the prophet Isaiah had told them that God took no pleasure in animal sacrifices made by wicked people. Instead, Isaiah told them, God wanted them to learn to treat other people properly.

The importance of the Bet Knesset probably dates from these meetings the Jews held in Babylonia. The meetings may have taken place outdoors or in private homes. Today we think of synagogues as big, impor-

The Bet Knesset probably grew out of the prayer meetings held by Jews in exile in Babylonia.

tant-looking buildings, but what is really important about a Bet Knesset is the people who gather there.

About fifty years after the destruction of the First Temple, the Babylonians were conquered by Cyrus the Great of Persia. Cyrus permitted the Jews to return to Eretz Yisrael. They soon built the Second Temple, where animal sacrifices resumed. But Jews of every community continued to meet in their local Bet Knesset.

In the Temple, the service and sacrifices depended on priests. Only people born priests could serve as priests. But in the Bet Knesset, every Jew was as important as every other Jew. Each Jew could study and become learned enough to lead services in the Bet Knesset.

When the Romans destroyed the Second Temple in 70 C.E., Jews mourned the loss. But they knew that no matter who conquered them or where they were forced to live, they could continue to worship God as a community in every Bet Knesset.

REVIEW IT

1. Name one good thing that resulted from the destruction of the First Temple.

2. Describe something good in your own life that resulted from an event that at first seemed totally bad.

Every Bet Knesset is a little Temple

For many Jews even today, the word "Temple" refers only to the two Temples of ancient times. All Jews, however, might call every Bet Knesset a little Temple. As you read more about why the Bet Knesset is considered a little Temple, ask yourself this question:

What three similar legends help explain why a Bet Knesset is considered a little Temple?

HAVE YOU HEARD?

The parliament of the State of Israel is called the Knesset (כְּנֶסֶת). Modern Hebrew has many other related words that suggest "gathering." Two of them are כֶּנֶס and כִּנּוּס, which mean "assembly" or "conference." The word for church, כְּנֵסִיָּה, also comes from the same root.

TEMPLE STONES AND THE BET KNESSET

The first legend is told about every Bet Knesset. When the Temple was destroyed, the story goes, God gathered its stones and scattered them across the earth. Wherever a stone fell, a Bet Knesset was set up. Because every Bet Knesset is made of part of the Temple, each Bet Knesset is considered a little Temple.

The second and third legends are told about the very old Bet Knesset in Prague, Czechoslovakia. The foundation of that Bet Knesset is said to be made of stones from the Temple. How did the stones get there?

According to the second legend, after the Temple was destroyed, angels carried away some of its stones on their wings. On the site in Prague where the angels placed the stones, a new Bet Knesset was built.

The third legend is slightly different. It says that some of the Jews who left Eretz Yisrael after the Temple was destroyed carried with them stones from the ruins. They had in mind the same Psalm that inspired Yehudah HaLevi to walk barefoot on the stones of Jerusalem: "Her very stones are dear to God's servants." When these Jews arrived in Prague, they used the Temple stones as the foundation of a new Bet Knesset.

Even though we know today of many a Bet Knesset that does not contain Temple stones, each Bet Knesset is still modeled on the Temple. For example, the Holy Ark is found at the far end of a Bet Knesset, just as the Holy of Holies was at the far end of the Temple. Also, each Bet Knesset is built so that the Ark faces Jerusalem, the site of the Temple. Perhaps your Bet Knesset even has the word "Temple" as part of its name.

REVIEW IT

1. Why is the Bet Knesset called a little Temple?

2. How can you behave in Bet Knesset to show that you consider it a little Temple?

HAVE YOU HEARD?

The second story also says that the angels told God they were taking the Temple stones to Prague "on condition" that they would return them to Jerusalem when the Temple was rebuilt. Since the Hebrew for "on condition" is עַל-תְּנַאי (äl tə•nī'), the Jews of Prague used these words as the name for their Bet Knesset. Over the generations, the similar-sounding Yiddish name Alt-neu (ält noi), meaning "old-new," was substituted. The Bet Knesset in Prague (shown above) is known as the Alt-neu shul to this day.

בֵּית מִדְרָשׁ

BET MIDRASH
bāt mid • räsh′

A **Bet Midrash** is a house (בַּיִת) of study or learning. A synagogue should be a Bet Midrash as well as a place for prayer.

Studying Torah is a lifelong activity.

CHAPTER FOUR

When you think of your synagogue, what sorts of activities do you think of? You probably think first of the activities that involve you, such as religious school classes. Because people of all ages study in the synagogue, it is sometimes called a Bet Midrash, or house of study.

Even if you have never heard anyone call your synagogue a Bet Midrash, you may have heard it called a shul. "Shul" is a Yiddish word that comes from the German word meaning "school." Jews have always thought of their houses of worship as places where studying and teaching take place.

In this chapter you will learn how important a role the Bet Midrash has played in Jewish life for thousands of years.

CHAPTER SUMMARY

Lesson 1: No one is too poor to study Torah.
Lesson 2: Jewish study is a lifelong activity.

Hillel and the Bet Midrash

Do you remember reading about Hillel, who taught his students that keeping themselves clean was a way of honoring God?

Hillel was not always an important leader. His brother was a rich merchant who wanted Hillel to go into business with him. But Hillel felt that business would leave him little time to study Torah. So Hillel became a woodcutter.

As you read about Hillel's struggle to become educated, ask yourself:

How did Hillel show his devotion to learning?

◄
Even though it was Shabbat, Shemaya and Avtalyon climbed onto the snowy rooftop to rescue Hillel from the cold.

HOW SHEMAYA AND AVTALYON SAVED HILLEL

As a woodcutter, Hillel earned a tiny income. He used half to support himself and his family. The other half he paid as an entrance fee to the Bet Midrash run by the teachers Shemaya and Avtalyon.

One wintry Friday, Hillel found no work. He had no money to pay his fee to the Bet Midrash. The guard at the door did not let him enter.

Hillel was so anxious to learn that, when the guard wasn't looking, he climbed up onto the roof of the Bet Midrash. He found a spot on the roof where, through a skylight, he could hear the words of Shemaya and Avtalyon. Even though snow began to fall, Hillel did not leave his spot because he was so eager to learn.

When the afternoon session ended, both the students and their teachers left the classroom to prepare for Shabbat. But Hillel did not come down from the roof.

Now, Shemaya and Avtalyon lived in another part of the same building where they held classes. The next morning, which was Shabbat, Shemaya noticed that there was less light inside the building than usual. Wondering about the weather, he and Avtalyon stuck their heads out the window.

Only then did they notice a figure on the roof, covered with snow. Even though it was Shabbat, when work is forbidden, they climbed up to the roof without any hesitation. They removed the snow that covered Hillel and brought him inside. Then they washed him and placed him in front of the fire. "For a man like this," they said, "we have no choice but to violate Shabbat."

From that day on, Hillel was allowed to enter the Bet Midrash without paying the entrance fee.

REVIEW IT

1. Why were Shemaya and Avtalyon willing to break the laws of Shabbat?

2. Name one subject you might be so eager to study that you would be willing to give up something you like in order to learn it.

Any place where Jewish study occurs can be thought of as a Bet Midrash. Here a special kind of group, called a ḥavurah, celebrates Purim by reading the Megillah.

Adult education and the Bet Midrash

Many people think that education is only for the young. The Jewish attitude has always been different. Teaching children is very important, but adults have a responsibility to continue learning as well. The story about Hillel, for example, shows that a Bet Midrash is a place where adults study. As you read about how Jewish adults have devoted themselves to Torah, ask yourself:

What examples from ancient and modern times show how important religious study is for Jewish adults?

BABYLONIA AND JEWISH STUDY

Ancient Babylonia, where the country of Iraq stands today, was a great center of Jewish learning. The Babylonian academies were famous for the classes they offered to the average adult.

Can you imagine 12,000 students agreeing to sign up twice a year for a month-long school session? That is what happened in Babylonia. The students included people who were farmers during the rest of the year. For one month during early spring and another month during late summer, they did not work in the fields. Instead, they attended lectures on Jewish law. The subject of each month-long session was announced in advance, so the farmers could prepare for the classes in their free time during the rest of the year.

Although most people today would take a different kind of spring or summer vacation, there are still many Jewish adults who continue the tradition of the Bet

In this Bet Midrash in Eretz Yisrael, immigrant children from India are learning about their new land.

Midrash. Your own parents may take part in adult education classes at your synagogue.

Any place where Jewish study goes on can also be thought of as a Bet Midrash. A major newspaper once had an article about a Jewish study group at a big-city law firm. A number of Jewish lawyers from the firm met regularly after work to study Jewish books. In that case, their office became a Bet Midrash after regular office hours. Similar Jewish study groups have started in many other cities.

REVIEW IT

1. How is today's adult Jewish study group like the twice-yearly courses at the Babylonian academies?

2. Explain why "Midrash" is the more important word in the term "Bet Midrash."

3. How might you continue your Jewish studies after you have reached Bar or Bat Mitzvah age?

גְּמִילוּת חֲסָדִים

GEMILUT ḤASADIM

gə • mi • loot' ḥä • sä • dēm'

Gemilut Ḥasadim means the performance of kind deeds. חֲסָדִים is the plural of חֶסֶד, which means loving-kindness. גְּמִילוּת comes from the word which means "reward" or "bestow."

Visiting a sick friend in the hospital is an act of Gemilut Ḥasadim.

CHAPTER FIVE

Cut into the stone wall of the B'nai B'rith Klutznick Museum in Washington, D.C., are the Hebrew words meaning "The world stands on three pillars: on the Torah, on worship, and on Gemilut Ḥasadim." These words have been put to music in order to help today's students learn this important lesson.

In this chapter, you will learn about the relationship between the ancient Temple and Gemilut Ḥasadim. You will also learn that Gemilut Ḥasadim includes many different kinds of kindness.

CHAPTER SUMMARY

Lesson 1: The Temple was built on a site made worthy by Gemilut Ḥasadim.

Lesson 2: We imitate God when we show Gemilut Ḥasadim to everyone.

Gemilut Ḥasadim and the Temple

Gemilut Ḥasadim played a role in the choice of where the ancient Temple would be built. But Jews do not need the Temple in order to practice Gemilut Ḥasadim. As you learn more about the Temple and Gemilut Ḥasadim, ask yourself:

(a) Where was the Temple built and why?

(b) What role did Gemilut Ḥasadim play after the Temple's destruction?

GEMILUT ḤASADIM AND THE TEMPLE SITE

Long ago, two brothers lived in Jerusalem. One brother was a family man, with a wife and four children. The other brother never married.

◄

According to legend, the Gemilut Ḥasadim shown by two loving brothers on Mount Moriah led God to choose that site for the Temple.

The two brothers owned a fertile wheat field on top of Mount Moriah in Jerusalem. They divided the work equally, and at harvest time they divided the wheat equally.

During one harvest period, the unmarried brother thought about the difference between his responsibilities and those of his brother. He said to himself, "I don't need as much of the wheat as my brother does. After all, he has a wife and children to support."

So, that night, while his brother slept, he took some of the harvested wheat bundles from his own share and placed them with his brother's bundles of wheat.

That same night, a troubling thought awakened the married brother. He realized that while his children would support him when he grew old or if he fell sick, his unmarried brother would have no children to care for him. He said to himself, "My brother needs more of the wheat than I do. After all, he has to be more concerned than I do about supporting himself in his old age."

So the married brother left his warm bed and went to the field. He took some of his wheat bundles and placed them in his brother's pile.

When morning came, neither brother understood why they still had an equal number of bundles of wheat. But neither said anything. Instead, each night during the harvest, each brother continued to place some of his bundles into the other brother's pile.

Finally, one night the brothers met in the field. Seeing each other's Gemilut Ḥasadim, they dropped the bundles of wheat they were carrying and hugged each other.

When it came time for God's House of Loving-kindness to be built, God chose the brothers' wheat field as the Temple site. The brothers' Gemilut Ḥasadim left its mark for all time on Mount Moriah, the place where they showed their brotherly love.

If you look carefully, you can find the Hebrew words גמילות חסדים carved into the wall of the B'nai B'rith Klutznick Museum in Washington, D.C. Compare the English inscribed here with the translation given at the top of page 31. How do they differ?

GEMILUT ḤASADIM AFTER THE TEMPLE'S DESTRUCTION

In the year 70 C.E., the Romans destroyed the Temple in Jerusalem. As a result, the Jews could no longer offer sacrifices to God.

One day, Yoḥanan ben Zakkai and his student Joshua stood in front of the ruins of the Temple. Weeping as he looked around him, Joshua said, "How awful that we can no longer atone for our sins by sacrificing in the Temple!"

Yoḥanan ben Zakkai comforted him by saying, "God told the prophet Hosea that He prefers mercy and loving-kindness to sacrifice. Surely we can still atone for our sins by Gemilut Ḥasadim."

REVIEW IT

1. According to the story, why did God choose Mount Moriah as the site for the Temple?

2. How was Yoḥanan ben Zakkai able to lessen Joshua's grief over the loss of the Temple?

3. Describe one way in which Gemilut Ḥasadim could improve your family life.

Imitating God through Gemilut Ḥasadim

Long ago, some rabbis were studying Torah. They wondered about the verse, "You shall walk after the Lord your God" (Deuteronomy 13:5). What could it mean to walk after God? The rabbis answered their own question in this way: Just as God practices Gemilut Ḥasadim, so should we.

The rabbis considered many different acts of personal kindness to be part of Gemilut Ḥasadim. For example, just as God provided clothes for Adam and Eve, so we should be sure to provide clothes for anyone who needs them. Just as God visited Abraham when he was recovering from surgery, so should we visit the sick. Read more about Gemilut Ḥasadim, and ask yourself:

How did Abraham learn the importance of showing Gemilut Ḥasadim to everyone?

SHOWING GEMILUT ḤASADIM TO NON-JEWS

The rabbis told many stories about how Abraham welcomed guests. For example, they described Abraham's home in Beersheba as having entrances in every direction so that travelers could easily enter. Not only did he feed the hungry, but he also gave clothes and money to needy guests. When guests tried to thank him, Abraham

Angered by the idol-worshiper, Abraham forgot to show his guest Gemilut Ḥasadim.

A single act of Gemilut Ḥasadim can benefit people in different ways. In this photograph, is the girl helping the elderly woman with her stitching, or is the woman helping the girl to learn a new skill?

would say, "Do not thank me. Thank God instead, for God gave me all that I have given you." In that way, Abraham taught his guests about God.

One night, an old man came out of the rain into Abraham's tent. Abraham washed his guest's feet, made a fire to warm him, gave him clean clothes, and fed him a meal.

After eating, the old man took an idol out of his bag and knelt down before it in thanks. Abraham said to his guest, "Aren't you ashamed to bow down before a piece of carved wood? Why don't you give thanks to the Lord Who created the universe?" The old man said, "I have always prayed to my own god, and I will not forget him in my old age." Angrily, Abraham forced the man to leave his tent.

These volunteers practice Gemilut Ḥasadim by taking part in a neighborhood cleanup drive.

Abraham went to bed but could not fall asleep. He heard God's voice ask him, "Where is the old man?"

Abraham answered, "I could not bear him and his idol worshiping any longer, so I drove him out of here."

God said, "I have put up with this man for more than seventy years, even though he does not honor Me. Couldn't you put up with him for even one night?"

Ashamed of himself, Abraham went out into the rain, caught up with the old man, and apologized to him. From that time on, Abraham showed Gemilut Ḥasadim to everyone, even those who refused to worship God.

REVIEW IT

1. What kind of Gemilut Ḥasadim did the rabbis praise Abraham for?

2. How did Abraham fail to "walk after God" in his treatment of the old man?

3. Describe two Gemilut Ḥasadim projects that your religious school class could carry out.

SEE FOR YOURSELF

Years later, when God gave His Torah to Abraham's descendants, Moses reminded the Children of Israel about the importance of showing Gemilut Ḥasadim to nonbelievers: "The Lord your God, He is God of gods. . . . He loves the stranger, giving him food and clothing. Therefore, you shall love the stranger, for you were strangers in the land of Egypt" (Deuteronomy 10:17–19).

דֶּרֶךְ אֶרֶץ

DERECH ERETZ
de'reḥ e'rets

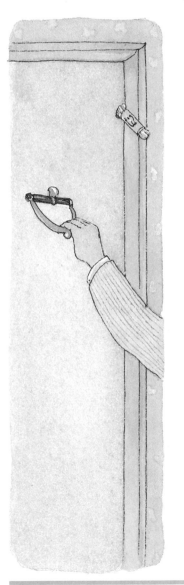

Derech Eretz means proper behavior, or the way that we are expected to act. דֶּרֶךְ is the Hebrew word for "path" or "way," and אֶרֶץ is the Hebrew word for "land."

Knocking before entering is a way to show Derech Eretz.

CHAPTER SIX

Derech Eretz includes many kinds of proper behavior. According to the rabbis, people can learn a lot about Derech Eretz by studying the ways of God described in the Torah.

For example, Adam thought he could hide from God after eating the fruit of the Tree of Knowledge. God called out to Adam, "Where are you?" The rabbis explained that of course God knew where Adam was. But God's question teaches one kind of Derech Eretz: not to burst in on someone suddenly.

In terms of your own behavior, think how much nicer it is to call up a friend on the phone to ask if you can come over to visit, instead of just showing up on the doorstep unannounced.

In this chapter you will read two stories that involve rabbis and Derech Eretz. In one story, the rabbi learns that Torah without Derech Eretz is meaningless. In the second story, the rabbi teaches his followers that sometimes Derech Eretz means showing less than perfect manners.

CHAPTER SUMMARY

Lesson 1: Torah scholars must set a good example by showing Derech Eretz.

Lesson 2: Respecting someone else's feelings is a kind of Derech Eretz.

Scholars must show Derech Eretz

Do you think your school would hire teachers who dressed sloppily or never washed their faces? Such teachers would not set a good example for their students. In the same way, the rabbis insisted that scholars follow the rules of Derech Eretz.

◄

There are many different kinds of Derech Eretz. We show Derech Eretz toward a flag—and toward the nation it represents—by displaying the flag properly and by saluting it in the right way.

The rabbis noted that if someone studies Torah, is honest in business, and speaks pleasantly to others, people then speak well of him and of those who taught him Torah. But if someone studies Torah yet is dishonest in business and treats other people meanly, what do people say about him? "This man studied the Torah, but he brings no credit to himself or to those who taught him!"

As you read a story about a Torah scholar who learned a lesson about Derech Eretz, ask yourself:

How did Rabbi Yannai learn the lesson that "Where there is no Derech Eretz, there is no Torah"?

WHERE THERE IS NO DERECH ERETZ, THERE IS NO TORAH

Rabbi Yannai once met a young man who was dressed like a student. He invited the young man to share a meal with him at his house. During the meal, however, Rabbi Yannai found that his guest was completely ignorant of Torah learning. He did not even know the blessings over the food.

Finally, in disgust, Rabbi Yannai said to his guest, "Can you at least repeat some words after me?" His guest assured the rabbi that he could.

"Then say, 'A dog has eaten Yannai's food.'"

The young man rose at this insult, and took hold of Rabbi Yannai. Shaking off the young man's grip, the rabbi said, "Can you explain to me why you deserve to share a meal with me?"

The young man answered, "Unlike some people, I've always been careful not to be rude. And whenever I come across two people arguing, I always try to make peace between them."

Rabbi Yannai suddenly realized how wrong his own

behavior had been. "How sorry I am for being so rude toward a man who shows so much Derech Eretz! How could I have forgotten the saying 'Where there is no Derech Eretz, there is no Torah'? We must not only study Torah, we must live Torah by acting decently."

REVIEW IT

1. What did Rabbi Yannai think was so important that made him behave rudely toward his guest?

2. Tell in your own words how the young man's response convinced Yannai of his own lack of Derech Eretz.

3. Make up your own story to show "Where there is no Derech Eretz, there is no Torah."

Derech Eretz in the modern world includes obeying traffic signals and waiting your turn.

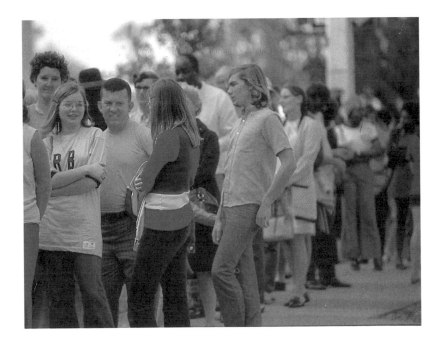

Derech Eretz sometimes means more than manners

Derech Eretz certainly includes good manners, but it also means showing special concern for the feelings of others. Here is another story that makes this point. As you read, ask yourself this question:

How did Rabbi Zev Wolf teach his followers that "Where there is no Torah, there is no Derech Eretz"?

WHERE THERE IS NO TORAH, THERE IS NO DERECH ERETZ

During Shabbat dinner, Rabbi Zev Wolf sat at the head of the table, surrounded by all his followers. The followers saw that the rabbi was deep in thought, so they spoke to one another in soft voices in order not to disturb him.

Now, Rabbi Zev Wolf was known for his kindness to strangers. Anyone was allowed to enter his house at any time, even in the middle of a meal. During this Shabbat dinner, a man entered and sat down at the table. All the other guests made room for him, even though they knew that the newcomer lacked Derech Eretz.

Soon after he sat down, the newcomer pulled a large radish out of his pocket. Then he picked up a knife from the table and cut the radish into many bite-size pieces. Finally, he began popping pieces of radish into his mouth, making a lot of noise as he chewed and swallowed each piece.

The other dinner guests were disgusted by the newcomer's lack of Derech Eretz. "You glutton," they said to him. "You eat like an animal in a barnyard, not like a guest at the rabbi's table. How dare you come here?"

Crunching on radish pieces may not be good manners, but in making the radish eater feel embarrassed, the other guests showed their own lack of Derech Eretz.

The rabbi's followers had tried hard to speak in low voices, but the rabbi soon noticed that the newcomer was being embarrassed. "Do you know what I feel like eating?" said the rabbi. "I would like nothing better than a really good radish cut into bite-size pieces."

The newcomer gladly passed the rabbi a generous handful of radish pieces. His happiness at being able to share something with the rabbi wiped away his feelings of embarrassment.

Later, after the visitor went away, Rabbi Zev Wolf may have said to his followers, "How would you feel if someone embarrassed you at my table the way you embarrassed the radish eater? I understand why you behaved the way you did. You felt he was showing no Derech Eretz. Unfortunately, the way you treated him showed no Torah. You must never forget the saying, 'Where there is no Torah, there is no Derech Eretz.' Good manners don't mean a thing unless they are based on concern for others."

REVIEW IT

1. How did Rabbi Zev Wolf's followers show him Derech Eretz? How did they fail to show Torah in their behavior toward the radish eater?

2. How can love for others be shown through Derech Eretz? Give two examples.

3. Make up another story in which a host puts a guest's feelings above proper manners.

זִכָּרוֹן

ZIKARON
zi • kä • rôn′

Zikaron, from the Hebrew word for "to remember" (זָכַר), means memory, reminder, or memorial. The Hebrew word זֵכֶר also means "reminder."

The Yahrzeit candle honors the anniversary of a loved one's death.

◄

CHAPTER SEVEN

The Zikaron of our slavery in—and Exodus from—Egypt is the basis for many of our Jewish holidays.

Jews believe that we can best live our lives in the present and the future by remembering our past. Throughout the year, we remember our past as a people in many ways. Reading the Passover Haggadah is one important way of reminding ourselves of our past as outsiders and slaves in Egypt.

In this chapter, you will learn about the Jewish responsibility to remember. You will learn why the Zikaron of our past in Egypt is so important in Jewish life. You will also learn how Jews keep alive the Zikaron of family members who have died.

CHAPTER SUMMARY

Lesson 1: The Zikaron of our past in Egypt provides the basis for many Jewish laws and practices.

Lesson 2: Jews keep alive the Zikaron of family members through special prayers and practices.

▲

A reunion of Holocaust survivors used a computer to keep track of those who disappeared or were killed during the Nazi period, so that their Zikaron could be kept alive.

The Zikaron of our past in Egypt

On the first nights of Passover, Jewish families read from the Haggadah. Shortly before we eat the seder meal, we read that we must all think of ourselves as having been personally freed by God from slavery in Egypt. As you read more about the importance of the Zikaron of our past in Egypt, ask yourself:

How does the Zikaron of our past in Egypt affect our behavior toward other people and toward God?

KINDNESS TOWARD OTHERS AND DEVOTION TO GOD

The Zikaron of our past as outsiders and slaves in a foreign land helps explain why Jews have always been concerned with doing things for other people. Again and again, the Torah teaches us to be kind not only to strangers but also to people who work for us because "you were a stranger in the land of Egypt."

It is important also to remember that it was God Who freed us from slavery. The Zikaron of the Exodus from Egypt is the basis for many Jewish holidays and for some of our basic feelings about God.

Passover　When Moses spoke to Pharoah in God's name, he repeated these words many times: "Let My people go so that they may serve Me in the wilderness." On the day of the Exodus itself, the newly freed slaves had their first chance to serve God by following the Passover laws.

Shavuot　Seven weeks later, Moses delivered the Ten Commandments to the people in the wilderness. We remember this event today by celebrating the holiday of Shavuot. The very first of the Ten Commandments states "I am the Lord your God Who brought you out of the land of Egypt, out of the land of slavery." This commandment is a kind of Zikaron.

Sukkot　The Zikaron of the Exodus is connected with a third holiday that Jews celebrate every year. The booths we build every autumn on Sukkot remind us of the tents the Israelites lived in as they traveled through the wilderness on their way to Eretz Yisrael.

Shabbat　Our past in Egypt is also connected with the holy day we observe not once a year but every week. People who were forced to work every day against their will should appreciate a day of rest once a week. As former slaves, we share the leisure of Shabbat with those who work for us.

Memory is really a way of keeping history alive. We can't be slaves in Pharaoh's Egypt (not that we would

HAVE YOU HEARD?

In the Kiddush for Erev Shabbat, we praise God for giving us Shabbat as a reminder of Creation—

זִכָּרוֹן לְמַעֲשֵׂה בְרֵאשִׁית

—as well as a reminder of the Exodus from Egypt—

זֵכֶר לִיצִיאַת מִצְרָיִם.

For Jews, remembering that God saved us is on a par with remembering that God created the world.

want to be), and we can't experience all the things that have happened to our people. But by remembering Jewish history we can apply lessons from our people's past to our own lives.

REVIEW IT

1. Describe one way in which the Zikaron of our past in Egypt should affect how Jews treat other people.

2. Explain how Shabbat is a Zikaron of our past in Egypt.

The Zikaron of our personal history

A Jewish cemetery in the Soviet Union. On the day of a Yahrzeit, some people go to the cemetery to visit their loved one's grave.

The next time you are in a supermarket, take a close look at the shelves where the kosher packaged foods are kept. Alongside the jars of gefilte fish, the boxes of matzah, and the bottles of borscht, you will probably find glass jars filled with wax and a wick, making a candle. Some people call gefilte fish, matzah, and borscht "Jewish soulfood." These foods are supposed to satisfy the Jewish soul. The Yahrzeit candles on the shelves next to these foods show that the Jewish interest in souls goes beyond food. Lighting these candles is one way we honor the memory of the people who have been important in our lives. Look for an answer to this question as you read on:

What customs do Jews observe in order to keep alive the Zikaron of those dear to them?

"MAY THEIR ZIKARON BE FOR A BLESSING"

In many congregations, every Shabbat the rabbi announces the names of members whose Yahrzeit will be observed in the week to come. The Yahrzeit is the anniversary of a person's death. After reading the list of names, the rabbi usually says זִכְרוֹנָם לִבְרָכָה — may their Zikaron, or their memory, be for a blessing.

Your parents love you all year long but pay particular attention to you on your birthday. In the same way, we may pay particular attention to the Zikaron of our dead loved ones on their Yahrzeit, even though we cherish their memory all through the year.

Many people make sure to go to synagogue for services on the day of the Yahrzeit. In that way, they can say the Kaddish (קַדִּישׁ) prayer as a memorial. Some people go to the cemetery to visit the loved one's grave. Many people give money to a worthy cause in the name of the person who died.

Several times a year, a memorial service is an important part of our worship. The memorial service is called Yizkor (יִזְכּוֹר), which means "May God remember." We ask God to remember the souls of the people who were important to us while they lived. In many congregations, the Yizkor service is recited on Yom Kippur, on the last day of Passover, and at the end of Sukkot and Shavuot. During Yizkor, many people pledge money to worthy causes in the name of their dead loved ones, זִכְרוֹנָם לִבְרָכָה. By helping others in the present we keep alive the Zikaron of important people from our past.

HAVE YOU HEARD?

"Yahrzeit" (yär′tsīt) comes from a Yiddish word meaning "year time," or anniversary. Yiddish grew out of a mixture of German, Hebrew, and other languages spoken by the Jews of Central and Eastern Europe. For centuries, Yiddish was the common language of millions of Jews in Russia and Poland.

REVIEW IT

1. When do the members of a family share the Zikaron of a loved one who has died?

2. When do all the members of a congregation share the Zikaron of loved ones who have died?

3. Is there a special person, now dead, who had an important part in your life? How can you best keep alive the Zikaron of that person?

יְרוּשָׁלַיִם

YERUSHALAYIM
yə • rōō • shä • lä'yim

Yerushalayim is the Hebrew name for Jerusalem. The rabbis taught that the name came from עִיר שָׁלוֹם, "city of peace."

The Damascus gate is a magnificent way to enter the Old City of Yerushalayim.

CHAPTER EIGHT

The rabbis felt that if all the beauty in the world were divided into ten shares, nine of those shares could be found in Yerushalayim. Many people living in modern Yerushalayim, shown in the photograph, would make that claim again today. But for many centuries between the rabbis' time and our own, Yerushalayim's ancient beauty was allowed to fade.

In this chapter, you will see some pictures that show why people have loved Yerushalayim for so long. You will also learn how Yerushalayim came to be the central city of Jewish life.

CHAPTER SUMMARY

Lesson 1: King David founded Yerushalayim as a city of peace.

Lesson 2: Yerushalayim has always remained at the center of Jewish hopes and prayers.

Yerushalayim, city of peace

According to the Bible, Yerushalayim fell within the borders of only two of the twelve tribes of Israel: Benjamin and Judah. But Yerushalayim was so important to all the people that a later legend assigned it to all twelve tribes. As you read a retelling of that legend, ask yourself:

How did David make Yerushalayim his capital?

YERUSHALAYIM AND KING DAVID

When David became king, he saw that Yerushalayim would be a good capital city for his kingdom. It was built on hilltops and could be easily defended. David seized the city from the Jebusites, the people who lived there.

◄
"Our feet stood inside your gates, O Jerusalem, Jerusalem built up, a city knit together" (Psalm 122:2–3).

Welcome to Yerushalayim, where each day brings an astonishing blend of old and new. Clockwise from top left: a bus trip starts your sightseeing tour; an Arab sheep market; the Dome of the Rock under a thin blanket of snow; archaeologists dig near the ancient Temple walls.

Clockwise from bottom left: Mea Shearim, the Orthodox section of Yerushalayim; brilliant sunshine lights the Golden Gate; fruits for sale at an open-air stall; ancient meets modern as television aerials sprout from Old City roofs.

But David did not want his capital to be founded through force. He wanted it truly to be a city of peace. So even though he had already won the city in battle, David offered to buy Yerushalayim from the Jebusite king for 600 gold pieces. The Jebusite king accepted the offer.

David now realized that if any single tribe bought the city, the other tribes would be jealous that the capital was not in their lands. Their jealousy might lead to arguments and maybe even to civil war. So David had each tribe contribute fifty gold pieces toward the purchase price. In that way, the twelve tribes each had an equal interest in the national capital. And Yerushalayim became the capital of Israel in a peaceful way.

Even though David thought about ways to keep peace, for much of his life he was a warrior. For this reason, he was not permitted to build God's Temple. That honor was saved for David's son Solomon, who had the First Temple built on Mount Moriah in Yerushalayim. King Solomon's name in Hebrew is שְׁלֹמֹה, which is related to the word for peace שָׁלוֹם.

This painted wooden model of Yerushalayim in a bottle was created in Germany during the nineteenth century.

WHAT TIME IS IT?

NAMES OF THE PEOPLE

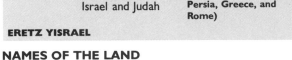

		JEWS		
Hebrews	Israelites	Judeans		Israelis

| 1200 B.C.E. | 1000 | 586 | 70 C.E. | 1948 |

| | Israel | Judea | Palestine | Medinat Yisrael |
| Canaan | Kingdoms of Israel and Judah | (Ruled by Babylonia, Persia, Greece, and Rome) | (Ruled by Rome, Arabs, Turks, and British) | (Independent State of Israel) |

ERETZ YISRAEL

NAMES OF THE LAND

The history of the founding of the United States capital is similar in one way to the legend about the founding of Yerushalayim. When Congress decided that the nation should have a permanent capital, the states began arguing about its location, since each state wanted to have the capital within its own borders. The solution was to place the capital within no state but on land that belonged to the federal government—the District of Columbia.

REVIEW IT

1. In what two ways did King David carry out his plan to make Yerushalayim a city of peace?

2. Give two examples from your own life in which one person completed a task begun by another.

3. Describe a time when members of your family avoided jealousy and arguments by sharing ownership and responsibility for something. If you can't think of an actual event, you can make up a story based on the idea of sharing.

Yerushalayim and hopes for the future

For many centuries, Jews have seen the return of the Jewish people to Yerushalayim as a sign of a happier future for all people. As you read more about the part Yerushalayim has played in Jewish hopes for the future, ask yourself:

How do Jews continue to treat Yerushalayim as a symbol of a happier future?

HOPES FOR A REBUILT YERUSHALAYIM

If you leaf through a prayerbook, you will notice that in every service we pray for Yerushalayim. We ask God to bring peace to Yerushalayim, and to let Torah be spread from Zion and Yerushalayim.

Prayers like these have been spoken by Jews over the ages. Every year, during the Passover seder and at the end of Yom Kippur services, we say, "Next year in Yerushalayim." Many Jews pray for Yerushalayim's future after each meal. The Grace after Meals (בְּרְכַּת הַמָּזוֹן)

asks God to rebuild the holy city of Yerushalayim speedily during our lifetime.

Even at a time when we are most happy in our personal lives, we think about the rebuilding of Yerushalayim. At traditional Jewish weddings, seven blessings are said over wine. The last three blessings ask God to comfort Zion, bring happiness to the married couple, and make joy complete by restoring Yerushalayim.

The peace of Yerushalayim is not meant just for Jews but for the entire world. The prophet Isaiah taught that a peaceful Yerushalayim will one day be a holy city for the people of a peaceful world.

REVIEW IT

1. Name two times when we mention Yerushalayim in our prayers.

2. According to tradition, how will the whole world benefit from a rebuilt Yerushalayim?

HAVE YOU HEARD?

The word "Zion," or צִיּוֹן, is pronounced zi'ən in English and tsi • yôn' in Hebrew. Zion is the name of a hill in Yerushalayim, but the name is often used to mean the whole city or even all of Eretz Yisrael. To read about an important political movement based on the idea of a Jewish state in Zion, see the chapter on Tzionut (pp. 117–22).

כְּבוֹד הַבְּרִיוֹת

KEVOD HABRIOT
kə·vôd′ hä·bri·yôt′

Kevod HaBriot means respect for our fellow creatures. כָּבוֹד is the Hebrew word for honor, and בְּרִיוֹת is the Hebrew word for creatures or human beings.

You can show Kevod HaBriot by helping the disabled.

CHAPTER NINE

You probably know the story that tells how Adam and Eve were driven out from the Garden of Eden. One version of this story says they disobeyed God by eating an apple from a tree that God had put off-limits to them.

But did you know that nowhere in the Torah is that fruit actually called an apple? The Torah gives an unusual name to the tree from which they ate: the Tree of Knowledge.

The rabbis explained that God did not want the descendants of Adam and Eve to know what kind of tree it was. God did not want people to curse the tree as the source of all of their problems. After all, the tree was part of God's creation! So to protect the honor of the tree, God did not let us know the real name of the tree from which Adam and Eve ate.

Just as God protected the tree's honor by not publicly shaming it, so must we protect the honor of our fellow creatures. The rabbis taught that shaming another person in public is like murder.

In this chapter, you will read three stories about Kevod HaBriot. In two of them, rabbis teach others important lessons about Kevod HaBriot. In the third story, you will read what actually happened when one famous rabbi publicly shamed another.

◄

Eyes shut and blindfolds on, the students in this classroom, guided by their blind leader, are trying to get a sense of what being blind might really feel like. Experiments like this one also let us experience even through our fingertips the wonder of God's Creation.

CHAPTER SUMMARY

Lesson 1: The custom of covering the ḥallah on Shabbat and festivals teaches a lesson about Kevod HaBriot.

Lesson 2: People with physical problems deserve Kevod HaBriot as much as anyone else.

Lesson 3: Even important leaders must practice Kevod HaBriot.

How covering the ḥallah shows Kevod HaBriot

Why do we cover the loaves of ḥallah on the Shabbat table? One creative way of explaining the custom is that by covering the ḥallah, we protect its feelings. Read the following story about some ḥallah that wasn't covered, and ask yourself:

How did the missing ḥallah cover help the rabbi teach his host a lesson about Kevod HaBriot?

HONOR PEOPLE BEFORE YOU HONOR THINGS

A Jew invited a famous rabbi to have Shabbat dinner at his home. All Friday afternoon the man's wife worked to prepare a wonderful meal, taking time out only to clean the house from top to bottom.

When her husband and the rabbi returned home from Bet Knesset, everything seemed in perfect order.

But as the man showed the rabbi to his place at the table, the man noticed that the beautifully braided loaves of ḥallah were not covered. In front of the rabbi, the man began to scold his wife for forgetting to follow the custom of covering the loaves.

As the woman's face became red with embarrassment, the rabbi rushed to her defense. "My friend," he said to the husband, "don't you know that the reason we cover the ḥallah is to protect its feelings? After all, we say Kiddush over the wine before we say the blessing over the ḥallah, and the ḥallah might feel second-rate if it saw the wine get its blessing first.

"Now," continued the rabbi, "if we are so concerned about the feelings of a loaf of bread, shouldn't we be even more careful not to hurt the feelings of our loved ones?"

Top: a ḥallah cover made in Germany during the nineteenth century. Bottom: an eighteenth-century German Kiddush cup.

REVIEW IT

1. Why did the man criticize his wife for not covering the loaves?

2. What did he learn from the rabbi's comments?

3. Look at the story about Rabbi Zev Wolf and the radish on pages 42–43. How is that story like this one?

Respecting people with physical problems

Moses had a speech defect. Yet he is one of the greatest figures in Jewish history. The Torah insists on protecting the rights of people with physical handicaps: "Do not curse the deaf, and do not put a stumbling-block before the blind."

Some rabbis wondered what was so bad about cursing the deaf, since they couldn't even hear the curse. The rabbis answered that deaf people too are created in God's image; if we curse them, we are also cursing God.

Read more about the honor we owe our fellow creatures despite their handicaps, and ask yourself:

How did Rabbi Eliezer ben Jacob teach others to respect the disabled?

RABBI ELIEZER BEN JACOB AND THE BLIND GUEST

Rabbi Eliezer ben Jacob once gave a dinner party. Among his guests was a blind man. To show the great respect he felt for the blind guest, Rabbi Eliezer ben Jacob gave the blind man the seat of honor at his dinner table.

Seeing how highly their host valued the blind guest, the other guests also treated the blind man with great respect.

The blind man understood what his host had done

SEE FOR YOURSELF

You can find the commandment to protect the rights of people with physical handicaps at Leviticus 19:14.

for him. He thanked the rabbi by blessing him: "You have shown love and respect to one who can be seen but cannot see. May you be rewarded with love and respect by the One Who sees but cannot be seen."

REVIEW IT

1. According to the rabbis, why is it wrong to curse someone who cannot hear?

2. Why is it wrong to treat any disabled person meanly?

3. In the story, who "can be seen but cannot see"? Who "sees but cannot be seen"?

4. Describe two ways of showing Kevod HaBriot to disabled people.

No leader is above showing Kevod HaBriot

In the two stories you have just read, rabbis used their influence over people to teach proper lessons about Kevod HaBriot. But there was a time in Jewish history when a very famous rabbi misused his power. When he failed to observe Kevod HaBriot, other rabbis took matters into their own hands. As you read a story about Rabban Gamaliel II, ask yourself this question:

What happened to Rabban Gamaliel II when he failed to show Kevod HaBriot to Rabbi Joshua?

RABBAN GAMALIEL AND KEVOD HABRIOT

In ancient times the Sanhedrin, the High Court of Israel, met in the city of Yavneh. The head of the Sanhedrin was given the title "Rabban" to show that he was more than an ordinary rabbi. He was head not only of the Sanhedrin but also of the famous Academy at Yavneh.

The chief justice of the Sanhedrin was Rabbi Joshua. He did not always agree with Rabban Gamaliel, but he was willing to accept Gamaliel's decisions.

Once, a student asked Rabbi Joshua if every Jew must say evening prayers. Rabbi Joshua told him that evening prayers were not required, even though it was good to say them.

When Rabban Gamaliel heard this news, he decided to use his power to teach Rabbi Joshua a lesson. At the next session of the Sanhedrin, Gamaliel announced his decision that evening prayers are required. He then demanded to know whether Rabbi Joshua had given the opposite opinion.

Rabbi Joshua admitted that he had disagreed with Rabban Gamaliel, but said he was willing to go along with Gamaliel's decision. Still Rabban Gamaliel was not satisfied. He forced Rabbi Joshua to remain standing throughout the whole day's session.

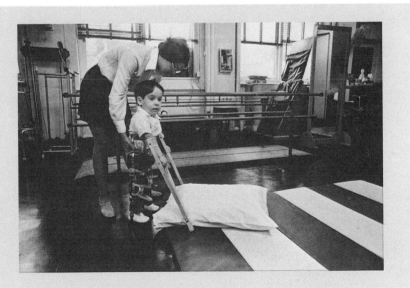

Disabled from birth, this young child is being taught how to walk.

All the other rabbis were upset by Rabban Gamaliel's behavior. At the end of the day, after Gamaliel had left, the members of the Sanhedrin met together without their leader. They decided to punish Gamaliel by removing him as head of the Academy at Yavneh.

When Rabban Gamaliel learned what the rabbis had done, he apologized to Rabbi Joshua for failing to show him Kevod HaBriot. Later, Gamaliel was given back most of his former honors.

REVIEW IT

1. How did Rabban Gamaliel fail to show Kevod HaBriot to Rabbi Joshua?

2. Make up a story about a camp counselor or teacher who acts toward a camper or student the way Rabban Gamaliel acted toward Rabbi Joshua.

The Torah insists on protecting the rights of people with physical handicaps.

כְּלַל יִשְׂרָאֵל

KLAL YISRAEL
kə • läl′ yis • rä • āl′

Klal Yisrael means all Jews everywhere. The Jewish community has many names: Knesset Yisrael (the assembly of Israel), Bet Yisrael (the house of Israel), and Am Yisrael (the people of Israel) are some of them. But when we say כְּלַל יִשְׂרָאֵל, we want to let people know that whatever differences we have, we share many things in common.

Klal Yisrael means forgetting our differences and joining together for a common goal.

The word יִשְׂרָאֵל begins with yod, the smallest letter in the Hebrew alphabet, and ends with lamed, the largest letter in the Hebrew alphabet. One explanation for this fact is that every member of Klal Yisrael has the chance to develop from a small child into an important person. As members of Klal Yisrael, we are encouraged to become the best people we can possibly be.

Sometimes we must put the needs of Klal Yisrael ahead of our own sense of importance. According to one story, when God told Moses he would die before the people entered Erétz Yisrael, Moses did not complain to God. He did not say, "I am such an important man. How can You do this to me?" Instead, his first thought was for the needs of the people. He said to God, "Please choose a leader to take my place, so the people will not be like a flock without a shepherd."

In this chapter, you will learn how all members of Klal Yisrael are connected with one another, with the Torah, and with God.

SEE FOR YOURSELF

Moses' plea to God to name a new leader for the people appears at Numbers 27:15–17. The new leader God chose was Joshua.

CHAPTER SUMMARY

Lesson 1: Acting together as Klal Yisrael, Jews can succeed where a single Jew cannot.

Lesson 2: The Wicked Son of the Passover Haggadah stands for Jews who choose to remove themselves from Klal Yisrael.

◄

Jews everywhere have given their encouragement, skills, and money to support the State of Israel and to help other Jews in need.

Working together as Klal Yisrael

How many times have you faced a task that you couldn't do on your own but that was easy to complete with the help of a few friends? The idea behind Klal Yisrael is similar: together we can achieve what may be impossible for any single one of us to do by ourselves. As you read about the meaning of Klal Yisrael in Jewish tradition and in the world today, ask yourself:

(a) *How are the members of Klal Yisrael like the letters of the Torah?*
(b) *What can we achieve through Klal Yisrael?*

KLAL YISRAEL AND THE TORAH'S 600,000 LETTERS

According to an old song, "Israel and the Torah are one," יִשְׂרָאֵל וְאוֹרַיְתָא חַד הוּא. Here is a way in which Klal Yisrael is like the Torah.

Tradition says that just as there are 600,000 letters in the Torah, so there were 600,000 Israelites in the Exodus from Egypt. That makes one letter in the Torah for every Jew! Without any one of those letters, the whole Torah would be different. Just as each letter of the Torah is of special importance, so each Jew has a special role to play in the life of our people.

KLAL YISRAEL CAN ACHIEVE GREAT THINGS

Sometimes it is hard to feel that the many different types of Jews in the world are all one people. Jews live in many different places and follow many different customs. In the United States, different groups of Jews have different religious practices. Also, some Jews are wealthier than others, and some are better educated than others. Often we tend to follow our own interests and don't pay very close attention to the needs of Jews who are different from us.

But whenever Jewish people are in trouble anywhere in the world, Jews always remember that they are part of Klal Yisrael. We forget the differences that separate us and band together to solve the problems.

The strength of Klal Yisrael has been proven many

times in the history of the State of Israel. Where Jews can, they give money. Those who do not have money often give their skills. And Jews everywhere give their encouragement. Today, Klal Yisrael also bands together to help the Jews in the Soviet Union, in Ethiopia, and wherever else the Jewish community is in need.

REVIEW IT

1. How are the individual Jews who make up Klal Yisrael like the letters in a Torah scroll?

2. When do Jews feel the need to band together as Klal Yisrael? In what ways can you show that you are a member of Klal Yisrael?

The Wicked Son and Klal Yisrael

When you first began your Jewish education, you may have learned one of Hillel's famous sayings: "If I am not for myself, who will be for me? But if I am for myself only, what am I?" You may also have learned another of Hillel's teachings: "Do not separate yourself from the community."

In the next section, you will learn how the Wicked Son in the Passover Haggadah selfishly stands apart from the community. When you finish reading, you should be able to answer this question:

How does the Wicked Son separate himself from Klal Yisrael while the Wise Son doesn't?

THE WISE SON AND THE WICKED SON

Every year at the Passover seder, we read about four different sons. First we meet the Wise Son. The Wise Son is curious about all the hustle and bustle of getting ready

A "run" is good fun and an excellent way for Jews outside the Soviet Union to raise money to aid Soviet Jews and focus public attention on their problems.

for Passover. He asks his parents, "What is the meaning of the laws and rules that the Lord our God has commanded you to fulfill?"

Notice that this son talks about "the Lord *our* God." He considers himself a member of Klal Yisrael, and is asking his parents to teach him how he can follow the Passover laws.

Next we meet the Wicked Son. This child is not at all like the Wise Son. He does not ask his parents a sincere question about the Passover laws. In fact, he has already made up his mind about them. He considers the Passover preparations nothing more than a big bother— for other people.

The Wicked Son says, in a nasty way, "What does this service mean to you?" By not mentioning God and by stressing that the laws mean nothing to him, the Wicked Son excludes himself from Klal Yisrael.

According to the rabbis of old, the Wicked Son is not really asking a question. For that reason, he does not deserve a real answer. The rabbis taught that if the Wicked Son had been a slave in Egypt, God would not have thought him worthy of being set free.

REVIEW IT

1. How does the Wise Son's question differ from the Wicked Son's?

2. What kind of answer would you give to the Wicked Son?

3. Do you think Klal Yisrael can or should find any way to include the Wicked Son and people like him? Explain your answer.

HAVE YOU HEARD?

The work of many Jewish organizations is carried on by members of Klal Yisrael. Every community has groups that teach people, run hospitals, and help the needy. This work could not go on without Klal Yisrael.

מְדִינַת יִשְׂרָאֵל

MEDINAT YISRAEL
mə • di • nät′ yis • rä • āl′

Medinat Yisrael means the State of Israel. Medinat Yisrael was founded on May 14, 1948, nearly 1900 years after the loss of Jewish independence in Eretz Yisrael (אֶרֶץ יִשְׂרָאֵל), the land of Israel.

Since 1948, this flag has flown over an independent Medinat Yisrael.

CHAPTER ELEVEN

The Declaration of Independence of Medinat Yisrael proclaims "the establishment of a Jewish state in the land of Israel." The Declaration refers to the history of the Jewish people in Eretz Yisrael. It tells how Jews continued to feel a special love for Eretz Yisrael, no matter where they lived. It describes how Jewish pioneers had recently returned to the land to rebuild it and to restore Hebrew as a spoken language there. The Declaration also talks about the Holocaust in which millions of European Jews were murdered. It suggests that if there had been a Jewish national homeland, the Holocaust would not have happened.

Two founders of Medinat Yisrael who signed its Declaration of Independence were David Ben-Gurion and Golda Meir. In this chapter, you will learn how they devoted their lives to the establishment and survival of Medinat Yisrael.

CHAPTER SUMMARY

Lesson 1: David Ben-Gurion was an outstanding founder and leader of Medinat Yisrael.

Lesson 2: Golda Meir earned a special place in the history of Medinat Yisrael as a searcher for peace.

◀

Prime Minister Golda Meir meets the press at a difficult moment in Israeli history: the Yom Kippur War, when Egypt and Syria launched a surprise attack on Medinat Yisrael.

David Ben-Gurion

Born in 1886, David Gruen grew up in Poland but developed a strong belief in the need for Jews to rebuild Eretz Yisrael. In 1900, when he was only fourteen, David helped found a youth group to encourage settlement in Eretz Yisrael. At the age of twenty, he himself settled there and took the name Ben-Gurion, which means "son of the cub." As you read more about David Ben-Gurion's work in founding Medinat Yisrael and in leading the new state, ask yourself:

How did Ben-Gurion help found Medinat Yisrael?

HOW BEN-GURION WORKED TO BUILD THE STATE

Ben-Gurion first worked in Eretz Yisrael in the orange groves and wine cellars of two Jewish settlements. He believed that a Jewish homeland should be based on the needs of its workers. At that time, Turkey was in control of Eretz Yisrael.

During World War I, Ben-Gurion learned that Great Britain had come to support the idea of a Jewish homeland. Ben-Gurion asked the British to form a Jewish Legion, a special Jewish army unit to free Eretz Yisrael from the Turks. After the Jewish Legion was formed, he joined it. The British soon took over control of Eretz Yisrael and much of the Middle East.

At first, the British suggested that Eretz Yisrael be divided into two states, one for the Arabs and one for the Jews. Ben-Gurion supported this plan. But the Arabs convinced the British that it would not be a good idea to set up a Jewish state in Eretz Yisrael.

When Adolf Hitler came to power in Germany, he threatened to destroy all Jews. But the British did not help Jews leave Europe to settle in Eretz Yisrael. Instead, they allowed fewer and fewer Jews to enter the country.

After World War II broke out, Ben-Gurion urged the Jews of Eretz Yisrael to help Britain win the war against the Nazis, but to resist the British limits on Jewish immigration. He suggested that they sneak as many Jewish refugees as possible into Eretz Yisrael.

After the war, the British refused to open up the doors of Eretz Yisrael to the European Jews who had

Above: the young David Ben-Gurion, during World War I, dons the uniform of the Jewish Legion. Right: about thirty years later, standing beneath a portrait of Theodor Herzl, Ben-Gurion proclaims the independence of Medinat Yisrael.

survived the Holocaust. Ben-Gurion visited the camps where these homeless Jews were kept. He promised them that, in time, every refugee who wanted to could come to Eretz Yisrael and help build a Jewish state.

Within a few years, the British decided to give up control of Eretz Yisrael. The United Nations voted on November 29, 1947, to divide the country into an Arab state and a Jewish state. The very next day brought an outbreak of Arab violence against Jews. The War of Independence had begun. Ben-Gurion raised money, collected arms, found military advisers, and prepared battle plans.

The Knesset, in Yerusha-layim, is the parliament of Medinat Yisrael. In order to gain and hold power, the prime minister must have the support of a majority of Knesset members.

When the British pulled out and Medinat Yisrael was proclaimed on May 14, 1948, Ben-Gurion became its first prime minister and minister of defense. He also helped found the Israeli labor movement and was one of its leaders for many years.

Ben-Gurion headed the government of Medinat Yisrael for most of the first fifteen years of freedom. He died in 1973. Today, people visit his house in the Negev, south of Beersheba, just as in the United States the homes of our most beloved presidents are popular tourist sites.

REVIEW IT

1. List three specific things David Ben-Gurion did to build Medinat Yisrael.

2. Why do you think Ben-Gurion changed his last name?

3. If you settled in Medinat Yisrael, what Hebrew last name might you choose?

Golda Meir

Golda Meir is the name this outstanding woman adopted in 1956, when she became foreign minister of Medinat Yisrael. She was born to the Mabovitch family in Russia in 1898, and was given the name Goldie. As a child, she lived through attacks by the Russians on the Jewish community. These attacks, called *pogroms*, convinced her at an early age of the need for a land that Jews could call their own. As you learn how she helped make this need a reality, try to answer this question:

What special role did Golda Meir play in helping to found and then lead Medinat Yisrael?

GOLDA MEIR'S SEARCH FOR PEACE

When Goldie was eight years old, her family fled the poverty and suffering they knew in Russia. They came to the United States and settled in the city of Milwaukee, Wisconsin.

But the young Goldie already had her own ideas about where Jews should live. When she was twenty-three, she moved to Eretz Yisrael with her husband, Morris Myerson. Soon she became very active in the labor movement that David Ben-Gurion had helped to organize.

Just four days before the founding of Medinat Yisrael, while Jews and Arabs were at war, Golda Meir was sent on a dangerous mission. She was taken across the border to meet secretly with King Abdullah of Jordan. She knew that if she were stopped by Arabs along the way, she would surely be killed. To hide her identity, she traveled to the meeting disguised as an Arab woman.

Golda's mission was to try to convince the King not to join the other Arab states in attacking Medinat Yisrael. Unfortunately, Jordan did join the attack.

HAVE YOU HEARD?

Golda once said that the greatest sin of Israel's enemies was not that they killed Israeli soldiers but that they forced Jews to learn how to kill.

In the government of the new state, Golda Meir held several important posts. She was Medinat Yisrael's first ambassador to Moscow, the capital of the Soviet Union. The Soviet government frowned on all religious practices. But when news of Golda's presence spread among the Jews of Moscow, they came in crowds to Moscow's Great Synagogue on the High Holy Days. The situation of the Russian Jews continued to concern Golda throughout her life.

In 1969, Golda Meir became Israel's fourth prime minister. As prime minister, she tried to achieve peace with the Arab states. But Egypt and Syria made a surprise attack on Medinat Yisrael on Yom Kippur of 1973. Her mission to make peace had been thwarted.

In 1977, when President Anwar Sadat of Egypt came to Medinat Yisrael, Golda Meir no longer held political office. Still, she did get to meet him and share her message of peace in face-to-face talks. She even gave Sadat a gift to honor the recent birth of his first grandchild. "As a grandmother to a grandfather, I give this to you," she said.

When Golda Meir died in 1978, the world learned that she had been ill for many years. The same kind of courage that made her willing to travel to Jordan disguised as an Arab woman made her able to bear secretly the pain of her illness.

REVIEW IT

1. What do you think was Golda Meir's most outstanding quality?

2. Why did Golda feel a special concern for Russian Jews?

3. Compare Golda's meetings with King Abdullah of Jordan and President Sadat of Egypt. What do you think accounts for the difference?

מִנְיָן

MINYAN
min • yän'

A **Minyan** is the number of people needed to hold a public prayer service. If a Minyan isn't complete, some prayers are not said. The word means "a counting."

"Nine rabbis don't make a Minyan, but ten shoemakers do."

CHAPTER TWELVE

Does your school have a student council where class representatives vote on school business? Your council may have a rule that a vote can't be taken at a meeting without the presence of a certain number of class representatives, known as a *quorum*. In a similar way, a Minyan is a quorum for Jewish prayer.

In this chapter, you will see that the need for a Minyan is related to some important Jewish values. You will also read two legends about the mysterious tenth member of a traditional Minyan.

CHAPTER SUMMARY

Lesson 1: The idea of a Minyan is connected with several important Jewish values.

Lesson 2: According to legend, great figures of Jewish history have come back to earth to complete a Minyan.

The Minyan and Jewish Values

An Orthodox Minyan must have ten males over thirteen years old. Many Conservative and Reconstructionist congregations count both males and females who have become Bar or Bat Mitzvah. In Reform congregations, a Minyan exists when any group wants to pray. But all four types of congregations honor the ideas that are connected with the Minyan. After reading the following, you should be able to answer this question:

How does the Minyan relate to basic Jewish values?

FOUR GOOD THINGS ABOUT A MINYAN

In Jewish tradition, the need for a Minyan is related to ideas about the holiness of God, Klal Yisrael, human worth, and growing up.

◀ Quorum calls are frequent in the United States Senate, for Congress is not allowed to vote on laws if enough members don't show up. Similarly, certain Jewish prayers normally aren't said unless a Minyan is present to say them.

God's Holiness   All Jews believe that the parts of a Jewish service dealing with God's holiness are special and require a full community to say the prayers. So traditional Jews don't say certain prayers that refer to God's holiness unless there is a Minyan.

Kaddish (קַדִּישׁ) and Kedushah (קְדֻשָּׁה) are two examples of such prayers.

Klal Yisrael   Sometime in your life you may have heard the saying "All members of Israel are responsible for one another."

Think about what happens whenever a member of your congregation loses a loved one. The other members of the congregation go to Bet Knesset or to the relatives' house to share the service with the friends and relatives of the person who died. So the Minyan shows the importance of Klal Yisrael and of the community.

Human Worth   Think about this saying: "Nine rabbis don't make a Minyan, but ten shoemakers do."

When it comes to completing the Minyan, it doesn't matter how educated, how religious, or how wealthy a Jew is. All have equal worth. The Minyan shows that every person has something worthwhile to give.

Growing Up   All Jews over the age of thirteen get to take on a new responsibility. Being old enough to contribute to a Minyan is a sign that you are growing up.

Two Jewish legends tell of a mysterious old man who arrives just in time to complete a Minyan. In the first legend, the stranger turns out to be Elijah the Prophet; in the second, the tenth worshiper is our ancestor Abraham.

REVIEW IT

1. Why is it customary to have a Minyan before saying Kaddish?

2. Once you become Bar or Bat Mitzvah, how will the Minyan give you a chance to help others and show your own value?

The honor of completing a Minyan

Jews have traditionally considered it both a responsibility and an honor to take part in a Minyan. But it has not always been possible to find the right ten people to make a Minyan. Legends have been told about the mysterious ways in which Minyans have been completed. As you read two of these legends, ask yourself:

What do the legends about completing a Minyan have in common?

THE MYSTERIOUS TENTH WORSHIPER

Hundreds of years ago, very few Jews were living in Yerushalayim. It was Yom Kippur eve and almost time to say the Kol Nidrei (כָּל נִדְרֵי) prayer, but only nine adult men were available. These nine men and their families had already gathered in the small Bet Knesset when, all of a sudden, an old man entered. His clothes were covered with dust, and he looked as if he had come a long distance. But no one cared how he looked. Everyone was delighted that on this holy occasion there would be a Minyan. To show their pleasure, the worshipers gave the tenth man the seat of honor.

The next morning, the stranger arrived early for services. Once again, he was given the seat of honor.

Each of the nine regular worshipers wanted to invite the tenth man home to break the fast at the close of Yom Kippur. But when they looked around after the shofar was sounded, they could not find him.

Only then did the members of the congregation realize who had completed the Minyan. It was none other than Elijah the Prophet. They named their Bet Knesset after him and kept his chair for many generations.

The second legend is based on the fact that the

Cave of Machpelah, the burial place of Abraham and Sarah, Isaac and Rebecca, and Jacob and Leah, is in the city of Hebron. Years ago, there were so few Jews in Hebron that they rarely had enough men for a Minyan.

One Yom Kippur eve, only the nine adult male Jews of Hebron gathered in the Bet Knesset.

Shortly before sunset, an old man entered. He was dressed in old clothes, his beard was long and white, and on his back he carried a traveler's pack. The residents of Hebron rejoiced to see him. Quickly, before the fasting and prayers began, they gave him a meal and a change of clothes. When they asked him his name, he answered, "Abraham."

The next night, after the fast was over, the nine regular worshipers drew lots to see who would be host to the honored tenth man. The lucky winner of the lottery left the Bet Knesset with Abraham at his side. But the next minute the old man was nowhere to be found.

Thinking he had lost his guest and would never see him again, the man of Hebron sadly broke his fast and went to bed with a heavy heart. No sooner had he fallen asleep than he began to dream.

In the dream, the old man appeared to him and said, "Let me tell you who I really am. I am your forefather Abraham, who first bought the cave in your town of Hebron. I saw how unhappy the Jews of Hebron were because they did not have a Minyan for Yom Kippur. For that reason, I joined you. Don't feel sad about my leaving. Let me assure you that this year will be a good one for you and the Jews of Hebron."

Tradition holds that these are the tombs of Abraham and Sarah, in the cave of Machpelah near Hebron.

REVIEW IT

1. Name two things the two legends have in common.

2. How do these two legends show how much Jews valued the idea of the Minyan?

עֲלִיָּה

ALIYAH
ä•li•yä'

Aliyah is the word used for the immigration of Jews to Eretz Yisrael. It means "going up." Jews who make Aliyah are called Olim, עוֹלִים —those who "go up." The honor of being called up to take part in the Torah reading is also called an Aliyah.

Each year, thousands of Jews make Aliyah to Eretz Yisrael.

CHAPTER THIRTEEN

I magine that you are walking down the street in one of Medinat Yisrael's large cities. How different the faces look from one another! The people in an Israeli city look so different from one another because many of them have made Aliyah from all over the world.

In this chapter, you will read about some dramatic events in the history of Aliyah. First you will learn what it was like to make Aliyah from Europe in the fifteen years before Medinat Yisrael was established. You will also learn how whole communities of Jews from Asia and Africa were brought to Medinat Yisrael.

As you read these stories, remember that not all Olim have stories as dramatic as those you will read here. Many families not too different from yours make Aliyah every year, as do many young people on their own.

CHAPTER SUMMARY

Lesson 1: It was very difficult to make Aliyah before Medinat Yisrael was founded.

Lesson 2: Operation Magic Carpet, Operation Ezra and Nehemiah, and Operation Moses have special meaning in the history of Aliyah.

◄

When the British rammed and boarded the refugee ship *Exodus 1947*, the Olim grabbed water pipes, bottles, sticks, jars of preserved foods, and other crude weapons in order to resist.

Aliyah Bet

As the Nazis came to power in Germany, the Arabs placed pressure on the British to slow down Aliyah. But the Jews of Eretz Yisrael nonetheless helped more than 100,000 European Jews make Aliyah. As you learn how, ask yourself:

What was Aliyah Bet?

ALIYAH BET: AN UNDERGROUND MOVEMENT

Adolf Hitler came to power in Germany in 1933. All European Jews were threatened. During the next several years, an underground movement began smuggling European Jews into Eretz Yisrael. The organizers called this underground movement Aliyah Bet. The aim was to bring more Jews into Eretz Yisrael than the British were willing to allow.

It was not easy for the leaders of Aliyah Bet to find ships to smuggle Jews out of Europe. Fuel and supplies were hard to get. From 1938 on, the British government used radar, patrol boats, and aircraft to keep track of Aliyah Bet ships from the time they left port till the time they approached Eretz Yisrael.

Once the ships were in British territory, the British felt free to attack. Sometimes they rammed the Aliyah Bet ships. Sometimes they used tear gas, sticks, or firearms against the Olim. Some ships were sent back. The passengers were taken off others and sent to British camps in Cyprus.

Even after the Nazis had been defeated and the war was won, the British refused to let more than a small number of Holocaust survivors enter Eretz Yisrael. But two events in Aliyah Bet history soon convinced the world that free Aliyah was needed.

In March 1946, the British convinced the Italians to prevent two ships from leaving an Italian harbor for Eretz Yisrael. Over a thousand Jewish refugees were on board. Although the passengers were already suffering from malnutrition after years in Nazi concentration camps, they went on a hunger strike to protest the British action. The world was horrified to see how British policy affected these survivors. The British had to let the two ships enter Eretz Yisrael.

In the summer of 1947, the most famous Aliyah Bet ship left a French harbor. The ship's name, *Exodus 1947*,

More than 1.6 million Olim have come to Eretz Yisrael since 1948. For every newcomer the government of Israel provides housing, education, and job training. Simple buildings like these provide housing for new immigrants.

recalled the Exodus of the Hebrews from slavery in Egypt. Over 4500 Jewish refugees were on board.

About twenty-four hours before the *Exodus* arrived at the coast of Eretz Yisrael, the British rammed the ship. A battle broke out. The Olim fought with whatever they could get their hands on—water pipes, bottles, sticks, jars of preserved food. Only after three people were killed and twenty-eight injured did the British manage to seize control of the ship and bring it to Haifa.

In Haifa, the British moved all the passengers to other ships and sent them back to France. But the French refused to help the British, so the Jews were taken to British camps in Germany—the country whose leaders had tried to kill every Jew!

The *Exodus 1947* incident helped convince the world that Britain's policy of forbidding free Aliyah into Eretz Yisrael was wrong. Less than a year later, the British left Eretz Yisrael, Medinat Yisrael was founded, and free Aliyah began.

REVIEW IT

1. Describe two events in the history of Aliyah Bet that prodded the British to give up control of Eretz Yisrael.

2. Why do you think the British were so determined to keep the Jews out of Eretz Yisrael?

3. How do you think the Israeli government should act if non-Jewish refugees need to find a country to take them in?

Famous Aliyah "operations"

Many Israelis made Aliyah from Europe or are descended from European Jews. But many are from the Middle East and Africa. Read on to learn how large groups of Jews from Yemen, Iraq, and Ethiopia made Aliyah, and ask yourself:

What roles did Operation Magic Carpet, Operation Ezra and Nehemiah, and Operation Moses play in the history of Aliyah?

HOW THE JEWS OF YEMEN MADE ALIYAH

For 2000 years, Jews had lived in Yemen. Under Muslim rule, they lived as second-class citizens.

Shortly after Medinat Yisrael was founded in 1948, the Yemenite ruler let all Jews wishing to leave Yemen sell their property and take their money with them. Most of the Yemenite Jews did not own much, and it was not hard for them to sell the little they did own.

More than 45,000 Yemenite Jews left their homes and were brought by air to Medinat Yisrael during 1949 and 1950. The Israelis gave the name "Operation Magic Carpet" to the Aliyah from Yemen. But to the Yemenite Jews themselves, Aliyah by airplane meant something else. They were reminded of what God told Moses to say to the Children of Israel: "You have seen what I have done to Egypt, how I carried you on eagles' wings and brought you to Me." To those who had never seen a plane before, the aircraft that carried them to Medinat Yisrael seemed like eagles sent by God to bring the Yemenite Jews to Him in the new Jewish state.

HOW THE JEWS OF IRAQ MADE ALIYAH

Iraq is a Muslim country on the site of ancient Babylonia. The Jews were taken as captives to Babylonia in 586 B.C.E., when the Babylonians destroyed the First Temple. About 150 years later, two Jewish leaders, Ezra and Nehemiah, led many Jews back to Eretz Yisrael.

Not all Babylonian Jews returned to Eretz Yisrael.

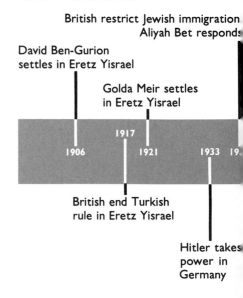

WHAT TIME IS IT?

British restrict Jewish immigration
Aliyah Bet responds

David Ben-Gurion
settles in Eretz Yisrael

Golda Meir settles
in Eretz Yisrael

1917

1906   1921   1933   19.

British end Turkish
rule in Eretz Yisrael

Hitler takes
power in
Germany

Operation Moses brought thousands of Ethiopian Jews to Eretz Yisrael, including these two children.

The Babylonian Jewish community flourished, and Babylonia long remained a great center of Jewish learning. In modern Iraq, however, conditions for Jews were never good. The Jews were forced to obey harsh laws and were often attacked.

In 1950, the government of Iraq allowed all Jews to leave the country. Unlike the Jews of Yemen, many Iraqi Jews had a lot of property. The Iraqi government made them sell all their goods at very low prices and let them take only a few dollars out of the country.

The Israeli government was able to move more than 121,000 Iraqi Jews to Medinat Yisrael. Most of the Iraqi Jewish community made Aliyah in a year and a half. The Israelis named this Aliyah of Iraqi Jews "Operation Ezra and Nehemiah," recalling the two leaders who had led many Olim from that part of the world more than 2000 years earlier.

HOW THE JEWS OF ETHIOPIA MADE ALIYAH

Rumors reached Europe for centuries about a tribe of Jews in Ethiopia, a country in northeast Africa. This tribe claimed descent from King Solomon and the Queen of Sheba. In time, the existence of this Jewish community became common knowledge.

The Jews of Ethiopia were called "Falashas," the word for "stranger" or "exile" in the local language. But they called themselves "Beta Yisrael," the House of Israel.

In the mid-1980s, there was terrible famine in Ethiopia. The government of Medinat Yisrael wanted to help the 25,000 Ethiopian Jews make Aliyah. But the government of Ethiopia wouldn't let the Jews go directly. Thousands made their way to a neighboring country, Sudan, and then were brought to Medinat Yisrael in secret airlifts. This Aliyah was named "Operation

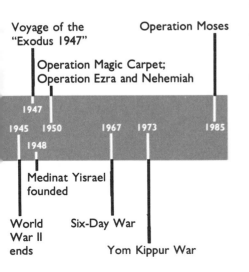

Voyage of the "Exodus 1947"   Operation Moses

Operation Magic Carpet;
Operation Ezra and Nehemiah

1947

1945   1950   1967   1973   1985

1948

Medinat Yisrael
founded

World   Six-Day War
War II
ends   Yom Kippur War

Colorful clothing and elaborate hairstyles mark the wedding customs of Israel's Yemenite Jews.

Moses." Just as Moses had asked Pharaoh to let the Hebrew slaves go free, so Israel and world Jewry were asking Ethiopia to let the Falashas go free.

Many members of Beta Yisrael arriving in Medinat Yisrael were uneducated and unfamiliar with modern city life. At the same time, others were university graduates. What a mixture of people found their way to Israel this time! While some knew all about modern machines, others had never seen a door or a window. All are finding hope in their new land.

REVIEW IT

1. Why do the names "Magic Carpet," "Ezra and Nehemiah," and "Moses" apply to these Aliyah operations?

2. Imagine that you are an Ethiopian child who has just made Aliyah in Operation Moses. List at least two ways in which you are probably different from a European Jewish refugee of the same age.

3. How has the Aliyah of Jews from different parts of the world helped Medinat Yisrael? What problems has it led to?

SEE FOR YOURSELF

When the Yemenite Jews compared the airlift to Medinat Yisrael with "eagles' wings" sent by God, they were thinking of Exodus 19:4. The stories of Ezra and Nehemiah are told in the Biblical books named after each.

עַם הַסֵּפֶר

AM HASEFER
äm hä • sā'fer

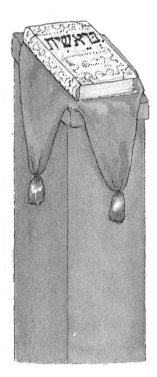

The Jews are sometimes called **Am HaSefer,** which means "the people of the Book." (עַם is one of the Hebrew words for "nation" or "people," and הַסֵּפֶר means "the book.") "The Book" originally meant "the Bible." But the Jews' devotion to reading has changed the way the phrase is used.

Books hold a special place in Jewish hearts and lives.

CHAPTER FOURTEEN

Jews consider books among their most valuable possessions and companions. If a prayerbook or Bible should fall by accident, an observant Jew will kiss it when picking it up. Jews would no more throw out their old and worn books than they would toss out an aged and sick friend. Instead, old books are taken to special hiding places in the attics or cellars of synagogues. From time to time, Jews bury the contents of these hiding places as solemnly as they would bury the greatest person who has died.

In this chapter, you will learn about the importance of books for Am HaSefer. In the first section, you will read a legend about a boy of long ago who learned to value books. The second section gives three modern examples of the Jewish love for books.

CHAPTER SUMMARY

Lesson 1: The study of Hebrew books offers many rewards.

Lesson 2: Am HaSefer's love of books becomes especially clear at times of crisis.

The importance of studying Hebrew books

Sometimes parents suggest that their children take up a certain hobby, like playing the cello. The children may turn up their noses and say, "Nobody I know would be caught dead playing the cello." But then something happens that makes the children change their minds. For example, they may discover that a friend is an expert cello player. As you read a story about a boy who learned a lesson about the importance of studying Hebrew books, ask yourself:

◀

The lines the Emperor wanted to hear came from the only Hebrew book the boy had ever learned— the Book of Genesis.

What did it take for the boy in the story to become a full member of Am HaSefer?

BECOMING A MEMBER OF AM HASEFER

This story takes place during the time when the Romans ruled Eretz Yisrael. A certain Jewish family had only one child, a son. Much to his parents' disappointment, the boy was not a good student. He thought that studying Hebrew books was something only his parents cared about. His teacher had a hard time teaching him anything. But somehow the teacher managed to teach him the first book of the Torah.

At that time, the Roman Emperor's soldiers sometimes stole Jewish children from their homes and put them in prison. One day, the Emperor's soldiers came to the town where the young student lived with his family. The boy was kidnaped by the soldiers and soon found himself in prison in another city.

It so happened that the Emperor himself came to that very city and visited the very prison where the boy was being kept. The Emperor asked the prison warden to show him the books in the prison library. As the Emperor looked through the books, he found one he couldn't read.

"This must be a book of the Jews," said the Emperor. "Do you have a Jewish prisoner to read it to me?"

The warden went directly to the boy's cell and said to him, "I hope for your sake that you can read Hebrew. The Emperor has summoned you to read a Hebrew book for him. If you fail, your head will be chopped off."

The boy swallowed hard and said to the warden, "Do you mean to say the Emperor himself thinks reading Hebrew is important? I could kick myself for having learned to read only one Hebrew book."

"Well," said the warden, "no matter. You must go to the Emperor at once."

Worn-out prayerbooks, Bibles, and religious objects are not just thrown away. Instead, they are buried with all the care and tenderness we show when a loved one dies.

The Shrine of the Book, in Yerushalayim, houses the Dead Sea Scrolls. Among these Hebrew and Aramaic writings, which were discovered in 1947, are the oldest known versions of the Book of Isaiah and many fragments of other Biblical books.

When the boy appeared before the Emperor, he breathed a sigh of relief. For the book the Emperor asked him to read was none other than the Book of Genesis, the first book of the Torah. The boy read and translated for the Emperor all of the first chapter and part of the second chapter, which describe how God created the world.

The Emperor then stopped the boy and said, "Your God has obviously brought me to this city and to this prison for the sole purpose of returning you to your family." The warden was told to give the boy silver and gold and to have the soldiers take him home.

When the rabbis heard what happened to the boy, they said, "This boy was taught only a single book, and God rewarded him and his parents. Imagine, then, how great a reward will come to a family whose children learn all the holy books."

REVIEW IT

1. Why did the boy resist studying the books of the Torah?

2. What finally convinced him that studying Torah was worthwhile?

3. Give two reasons why you think it is important for Jewish children today to study Jewish books.

Am HaSefer in times of crisis

The legend you just read is set in the ancient world. But in the modern world, too, the Jewish love for books has been made clear time after time. As you read three dramatic examples from our own century of how Am HaSefer has treasured books, ask yourself:

How have modern Jews shown their love and respect for books during times of war and oppression?

BOOKS AND THE HOLOCAUST

During World War II, many Jewish communities in Europe were wiped out. Six million Jews were murdered by the Nazis.

After the war, the survivors from the different Jewish towns and villages wanted to honor the dead in some lasting way. After all, the victims had not received proper burials, and so had no gravestones.

Some of the survivors revived an old Jewish custom. They wrote down the history of the Jews of their communities. The books that contain this history are called "Yizkor Books," or memorial books. More than 500 Yizkor Books were written to preserve the history of the Jewish communities the Nazis had destroyed.

Many of the writers of the Yizkor Books were not educated people. But as members of Am HaSefer they understood the power of books to keep alive the memory of the lost communities.

BOOKS AND THE HEBREW UNIVERSITY

Before the War of Independence began in 1947, the Hebrew University of Jerusalem was located on Mount Scopus. After the war, that area was under Jordanian control.

The Israelis set up temporary buildings for the university in the part of Yerushalayim that was under their control. But what kind of university could it be without its collection of books?

The Jordanian government posted Arab guards to keep the Israelis from removing more than a small number of books from Mount Scopus. But the Israelis could not be satisfied with less than the entire library. So Israeli guards, who were there to prevent looting, smuggled books past the Arab guards.

Travelers to the Soviet Union often pack books and religious items that will help Soviet Jews live Jewish lives.

Some people think the Arab guards knew that the contents of the old library were slowly finding their way to Israeli-held Jerusalem. The Arabs had been the first to give the name "the people of the Book" to the Jews. Perhaps this history explains why they let the Israelis secretly restore the library on the other side of town.

BOOKS AND SOVIET JEWS

It is difficult for the Jews of the Soviet Union today to observe Jewish holidays and customs. They find it even more difficult to get Jewish books for their homes and groups.

Some American Jews who visit the Soviet Union make sure to bring with them books that teach Jewish ideas and the Hebrew language. They also bring other items that will make it easier for Soviet Jews to live Jewish lives.

The Soviet government forbids tourists from bringing in such books and religious items except for their own personal use. But both the tourists and the Soviet Jews are willing to risk arrest and prison because books are so important to Am HaSefer.

REVIEW IT

1. What is a Yizkor Book?

2. Describe two times in modern Jewish history when Jews have been involved in book smuggling.

3. If you were forbidden to read, what would your reaction be?

HAVE YOU HEARD?

Some Jews in the Soviet Union are called "refuseniks." This is because their requests for permission to leave the Soviet Union for Israel have been refused by the Soviet government.

פִּקּוּחַ נֶפֶשׁ

PIKUAH NEFESH
pi • kōō′aḥ ne′fesh

Pikuah Nefesh means "saving a life." The duty of saving a life is more important than nearly all the other Mitzvot.

Pikuaḥ Nefesh means "saving a life."

Our Father in heaven, You know we
would like to observe the festival of
Passover by eating Matzah and not eating
Ḥametz. But we cannot, and therefore our
hearts are sad: our enslavement prevents
us, for our lives are in danger. Behold,
then, we are ready to fulfill Your
commandment of "You shall live by them
and not die by them." We pray that You
will keep us alive and redeem us so that
we may observe Your laws and serve You
with a perfect heart. Amen.

CHAPTER FIFTEEN

The prayer you see on the facing page is not a traditional one. You are taught to say a blessing before doing a Mitzvah. But Jews in a Nazi concentration camp were taught by their religious leaders to say a prayer like this one before *breaking* a Mitzvah.

The laws of Passover require that Jews not eat leavened foods during the holiday. But the rabbis in the concentration camp told the Jews that they must eat leavened foods in order to survive. In other words, Pikuah Nefesh was more important than the Mitzvah of eating only unleavened foods on Passover.

In this chapter you will read two stories about Pikuah Nefesh. The first story shows that Pikuah Nefesh is more important than Shabbat laws. The second story shows that saving human lives is more important than the laws of Yom Kippur.

◄

In the Nazi concentration camps at Passover time, the Jews faced a difficult choice. Since there was no Matzah, they had to choose whether to eat Hametz, and so break the laws of Passover; or to eat nothing, and so violate the commandment of Pikuah Nefesh. The prayer you see reflects the fact that Pikuah Nefesh is more important than nearly all the other Mitzvot.

CHAPTER SUMMARY

Lesson 1: The laws of Shabbat can be broken only in order to save lives.

Lesson 2: The laws of Yom Kippur must be suspended in order to save human lives.

Pikuah Nefesh and Jewish law

One of the Shabbat laws forbids writing during the day of rest. When Rosh HaShanah was scheduled to fall on Shabbat one year, Rabbi Levi Yitzhak of Berditchev was worried. On Rosh HaShanah we ask God to write our names in the Book of Life. But how could God do so on a day when writing was forbidden? Read on to see how the rabbi solved the problem and ask yourself:

How did Rabbi Levi Yitzhak try to save Jewish lives by telling God how to break one of His own Mitzvot?

ROSH HASHANAH, SHABBAT, AND THE BOOK OF LIFE

Rabbi Levi Yitzḥak thought long and hard about the problem of how God could write the names of Jews in any of the three books opened on Rosh HaShanah: the Book of Life (reserved for the perfectly pious), the Book of Death (reserved for the perfectly wicked), or the third book (for all those who are neither perfectly good nor perfectly bad). There seemed to be a conflict between the laws of Shabbat, which demanded that God not write, and the tradition of Rosh HaShanah, which demanded that every Jew's name be written in one of the three books.

Finally, as Shabbat and Rosh HaShanah both began, the rabbi saw a way around the problem. Levi Yitzḥak was known for his boldness in speaking to God on behalf of the Jews. On this occasion he made one of his boldest pleas:

"Master of the Universe! As you know, Pikuaḥ Nefesh is more important than the Shabbat laws. In order

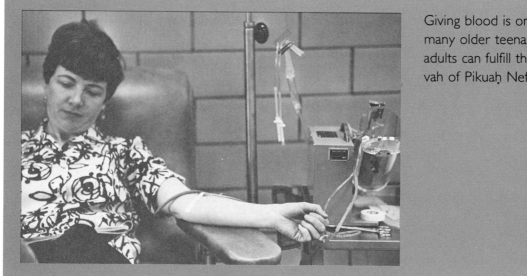

Giving blood is one way many older teenagers and adults can fulfill the Mitzvah of Pikuaḥ Nefesh.

to save human lives, we are not only allowed to break Shabbat laws, we are actually required to do so. The rabbis of old taught that it is a Mitzvah to break the Shabbat in order to save a life, and the more eager one is to do so, the more praise one deserves.

"So, Master of the Universe, You have only one choice today. If You are going to break the Shabbat laws by writing anything today at all, You must inscribe the entire people of Israel for a year of life. I expect You to set a good example for Your people by violating the Shabbat laws only to save human lives."

REVIEW IT

1. Explain in your own words the logic behind Rabbi Levi Yitzḥak's reasoning.

2. Why might God have done what Levi Yitzḥak insisted on?

3. Go over the story of how Shemaya and Avtalyon saved Hillel on Shabbat (pages 25–26). What does this story have to do with Pikuaḥ Nefesh?

Pikuaḥ Nefesh and Yom Kippur

Just as it is a Mitzvah to break Shabbat laws in order to save a life, it is also a Mitzvah to violate the laws of Yom Kippur when lives are at stake. As you read a famous story about a rabbi who dramatically showed the importance of Pikuaḥ Nefesh, look for an answer to this question:

What phrase from the Bible did the rabbi quote to prove to the congregation that they must eat on Yom Kippur that year?

WHEN JEWS MUST EAT ON YOM KIPPUR

One summer many years ago, an epidemic of cholera spread throughout Eastern Europe. Every family was affected. Many people died.

As the summer drew to a close, the epidemic continued to rage. This is the story of what happened on Yom Kippur in one small Jewish town that was especially hard-hit.

Following Kol Nidrei in the Yom Kippur service, the white-haired rabbi did not give a sermon, as was his custom. Instead, he read a long list of names — the names of the Jews who had died that week. There were many more names on the list than worshipers in the room. Then the rabbi led the memorial service for the dead — Yizkor.

No one left the Bet Knesset that night. People wept and prayed and wept some more. Early that morning, the congregation noticed that two of the worshipers had died while praying.

Still the prayers went on. Then, in the afternoon, the rabbi began his long-awaited sermon.

"Dear friends, God told Moses to say to our ancestors that whoever observes the Mitzvot 'shall live by them.' Our rabbis understood this to mean that if observing a Mitzvah endangers a person's life, the Mitzvah must not be observed. We must always put our lives ahead of the Torah."

The rabbi then recited these words: "With the consent of God and with the consent of the congregation, we declare it lawful to eat and drink today."

The silence that filled the room was so complete that it seemed as if the worshipers had stopped breathing, as if their hearts had stopped beating. Then, as the meaning of the rabbi's words sank in, the congregation began to weep. Even the rabbi broke down and wept.

SEE FOR YOURSELF

The idea that people should live by the Mitzvot, not die by them, comes from Leviticus 18:5.

Through his tears, the rabbi spoke in a soft voice. "I know, my friends, how hard it is for you to violate Yom Kippur. Do you think it will be easy for me? Today is my eightieth birthday. Up until now, I have never knowingly violated a Mitzvah. But Pikuaḥ Nefesh is also a Mitzvah. Our rabbis taught: 'Any law must be suspended even when there is only a possible danger to human life.' We all know that the epidemic strikes those who are made weak by hunger and thirst. It is God's will that we eat this year on Yom Kippur."

The rabbi then ordered that a tray of cookies and wine be brought to the Bet Knesset. The rabbi was the first to eat. "I have set an example for you all," he said. "May God's name be blessed."

Many members of the congregation then ate and drank, washing down the cookies and wine with their tears.

"We declare it lawful to eat and drink today," the rabbi said on Yom Kippur.

The duty of Pikuaḥ Nefesh is recognized throughout the world, among both Jews and non-Jews. Fire-fighters everywhere daily risk their lives so that others may live.

REVIEW IT

1. Why were the Jews in the story urged to eat on Yom Kippur? Who urged them to eat?

2. Why do you think the members of the congregation, who understood the meaning of Pikuaḥ Nefesh, were so unhappy about doing what the rabbi was telling them to do?

3. What might convince you to give up an important custom in your own life?

צְדָקָה

TZEDAKAH
tsə • dä • kä'

Most people would say that **Tzedakah** means "charity," but actually the word comes from צֶדֶק, the Hebrew term for "justice." All Jews—even those who receive Tzedakah themselves—have the duty to give Tzedakah to those who are in need.

Thousands of Tzedakah boxes just like this one have collected millions of dollars for the Jewish National Fund.

▲
Top: a brass Tzedakah box, made in Eastern Europe. Bottom: a German Tzedakah box, crafted in silver.

◄
The highest form of Tzedakah is teaching people how to provide for their own needs. Here Moroccan Jews are learning computer skills.

I n your Jewish school, you have probably seen a metal box like one of those shown on page 111. Maybe your family keeps one at home. At school or at home, boxes like these—plain or fancy, old-fashioned or modern—are used to collect Tzedakah money. When a Tzedakah box is filled, its contents are sent to groups that help Jews or other needy people in the United States and in other countries around the world.

In this chapter you will learn how Rabbi Akiba taught another great rabbi the importance of Tzedakah. You will also learn why Tzedakah is as important as saying prayers.

CHAPTER SUMMARY

Lesson 1: A great rabbi had to be taught the importance of Tzedakah.

Lesson 2: Sometimes Tzedakah is even more important than faith in God.

The importance of giving Tzedakah

Rabbi Tarfon has gone down in history as a generous man who used his great wealth to help the needy. But he was not always so generous. After you read the following story, you should be able to explain:

How did Rabbi Akiba teach Rabbi Tarfon the importance of Tzedakah?

TZEDAKAH AND RABBI TARFON

Rabbi Tarfon was a scholar like his friend, the great Rabbi Akiba. He knew the Torah's teaching that we must "open our hands" and not "harden our hearts" to the poor. In addition, he was a rich man. But despite his knowledge of Torah and despite his wealth, Tarfon did not fulfill his duty of giving Tzedakah to the poor.

Rabbi Akiba was worried about Rabbi Tarfon's lack of concern for needy people. One day, Akiba said to Tarfon, "If you give me 4000 pieces of gold, I will buy a town or two for you. You will not regret making the investment I have in mind."

Rabbi Tarfon willingly gave the money to Rabbi Akiba. But instead of buying buildings and land with the money, Akiba gave the coins to needy students of Torah.

Some time later, Rabbi Tarfon asked Rabbi Akiba to show him the towns the 4000 pieces of gold had bought. Much to Tarfon's surprise, Akiba led him to the house of study—the Bet Midrash—where the needy students sat and studied Torah.

"I don't understand, Akiba," said Rabbi Tarfon. "You said you were going to buy me some real estate. Show me what I have gotten for my money. No sensible person gives his money away for nothing."

Then Rabbi Akiba said, "This is the city I have bought for you, Rabbi Tarfon! You will benefit from this investment not only in this world but also in the world to come."

Rabbi Tarfon turned to Rabbi Akiba and said, "You are my master in wisdom and my guide in proper conduct." And he handed Rabbi Akiba another large sum of money to give to the poor.

Instead of buying towns, Rabbi Akiba used Rabbi Tarfon's money to make a better investment—to support needy students of Torah.

REVIEW IT

1. Where did Rabbi Tarfon expect Rabbi Akiba to take him? Why was he surprised?

2. In what way were the needy Torah students like a real estate investment? In what way were they different?

Tzedakah, the Angels, and God

Rabbi Tarfon is not the only person in history who has found it difficult to give money to others. It seems that people always have an excuse for putting off the Mitzvah of Tzedakah. Sometimes they even use their faith in God as an excuse! To see how, read the following stories and ask yourself:

(a) Why can collecting Tzedakah be called a greater Mitzvah than singing hymns of praise to God?

(b) Why should a Jew give Tzedakah as if there were no God?

COLLECTING TZEDAKAH OR RECITING PSALMS?

A pious Jew once decided to spend the whole day chanting the Book of Psalms. Toward evening, he was interrupted by a messenger from his rabbi. The rabbi, said the messenger, wanted to see the man at once.

The pious Jew thought to himself, "The rabbi probably wants me to do something if he is calling for me so urgently. But not even the rabbi is going to stop me."

So the Jew instructed the messenger to tell the rabbi that he would come as soon as he had finished with all the Psalms.

After a short time, the messenger returned, saying the rabbi wanted the pious man to put aside the Psalms and come immediately. This time the Jew did as the rabbi asked.

"Why didn't you come when I called you the first time?" asked the rabbi.

The Jew explained that he had been busy chanting hymns of praise to God. The rabbi then said, "I called you to collect Tzedakah for a needy Jew. The Angels can sing God's praises, but people are needed to collect Tzedakah for the poor. Collecting Tzedakah is a greater Mitzvah than chanting Psalms, because the Angels cannot perform Tzedakah."

TZEDAKAH AND NOT BELIEVING IN GOD

Rabbi Moshe Leib of Sassov once said, "God created every human thought and feeling for a holy purpose."

One of the rabbi's students asked, "But rabbi, what about someone who thinks God does not exist? Is this a thought with a holy purpose?"

The rabbi answered, "The Mitzvah of Tzedakah proves that even thinking God doesn't exist can serve a holy purpose. If a needy person comes to a person who believes in God and asks for help, that person might be tempted to say, 'God will provide for you. There's no need for me to give you Tzedakah.'

"When it comes to giving Tzedakah," continued Rabbi Moshe Leib, "every Jew should act as if there were no God to help the needy. Every man and every woman must aid the poor as if he or she were their only source of help."

REVIEW IT

1. Explain how each story shows that people must *do* something to help other people, rather than rely on prayers or faith.

2. When do you most like giving to Tzedakah projects? When would you rather have your parents give for you?

In Yerushalayim, two young women give Tzedakah to a blind Arab beggar.

HAVE YOU HEARD?

Your Tzedakah goes to many different groups. These groups feed the hungry, clothe the poor, support Aliyah, help people with problems, provide medical aid, and create exciting new projects for Jews throughout the United States.

צִיּוֹנוּת

TZIONUT

tsi • yô • no͞ot′

Tzionut is the Hebrew word for Zionism. Tzionut takes its name from צִיּוֹן or Zion, the name of one of the hills in Yerushalayim. The name "Zion" has often been used in poetry to stand for the whole city and even for the whole of Eretz Yisrael.

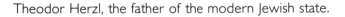

Theodor Herzl, the father of the modern Jewish state.

CHAPTER SEVENTEEN

Tzionut began as a movement to establish an independent Jewish state. Since the creation of Medinat Yisrael in 1948, the movement has continued to support the Jewish state. People who support Tzionut are called Zionists. Zionists have brought people from all over the world to create a state the Jewish people can truly call home.

The growth of one of the leading cities in Medinat Yisrael tells a great deal about the success of Tzionut. In 1909 a group of early Zionists from Russia stood in the sands near the ancient seaport of Jaffa. They gathered there to found a new Jewish city, called Tel Aviv. By the 1980s, Tel Aviv had grown from a cluster of sand dunes into one of the world's great cities. More than a million people now live in the district that includes Tel Aviv and the modern port city of Jaffa.

In this chapter, you will learn about the history of Tzionut and about its present programs.

◀

Each year on Yom Ha-Atzma'ut—Israel's Independence Day—we celebrate the triumph of Tzionut and the founding of the Jewish state. Notice how the photographer has captured the whir of excitement at this Independence Day celebration, which took place in Yerushalayim in 1968, less than a year after the city had been reunited during the Six-Day War.

CHAPTER SUMMARY

Lesson 1: Theodor Herzl was the father of the modern Jewish state.

Lesson 2: Zionist groups today unite Jews from all over the world in their support for Medinat Yisrael.

Theodor Herzl: Father of the modern Jewish state

Americans are expected to know that George Washington was the father of their country. Jews should also know about the father of the modern Jewish state. Unlike George Washington, the father of the Jewish state did not live to see the birth of the country he fought for. As you read more about the role Theodor Herzl played in the early Zionist movement, ask yourself:

Why is Herzl considered the father of Tzionut?

This classic portrait captures Herzl in a thoughtful mood.

"IF ONLY YOU WILL IT, IT IS NO DREAM"

Born in 1860 in the European city of Budapest, Theodor Herzl became a lawyer, writer, and newspaper reporter. At the age of thirty-four, he was assigned to cover the trial in Paris of Alfred Dreyfus, a captain in the French army. Dreyfus, a Jew, was falsely accused of selling military secrets to Germany. In 1894 a military court found Dreyfus guilty and sentenced him to life in prison.

Anti-Jewish riots broke out in France. Like other Jews, Herzl was shocked by the Dreyfus Affair. Herzl had never before given much thought to his Jewishness. Herzl knew that, for a century, Jews living in France had enjoyed the same rights as other French citizens. If such strong anti-Jewish feelings could break out in France because of a faked case against one Jewish army officer, then Jews everywhere were in serious trouble.

Herzl's solution to this problem was the founding of a Jewish state. To work out the details, Herzl called a meeting of the first Zionist World Congress in Switzerland. Herzl predicted that within fifty years of the meeting, held in 1897, there would be a Jewish state.

After a trip to Eretz Yisrael, Herzl wrote a novel about a modern Jewish state there. He ended the book with the words, "If only you will it, it is no dream." These words became the slogan of the Zionist movement.

For the rest of his short life, Herzl devoted himself to the cause of Tzionut. Herzl was only in his early forties when he died in 1904. The father of the Jewish state did not live to see it born in 1948, although he had come close to predicting its birthdate exactly.

REVIEW IT

1. What event made Herzl turn to Tzionut as an answer to Jewish problems?

2. What phrase of Herzl's became the slogan of Tzionut?

Zionist organizations today

Do you or your parents think of yourselves as Zionists? The chances are good that you or other members of your family support some Zionist groups. After you read more about some of these groups, you should be able to answer this question:

How do different Zionist groups support Israel?

SUPPORTING MEDINAT YISRAEL

Your mother may be a member of *Hadassah*, the Women's Zionist Organization of America. Hadassah is the world's largest grouping of Jewish women.

Hadassah is older than Medinat Yisrael by more than thirty years. Before the founding of the Jewish state, Hadassah helped improve health conditions in Eretz Yisrael. It also helped rescue children from Nazi Germany and settle them in Eretz Yisrael.

Today, much of the money collected by Hadassah supports hospitals and health research in Israel. The Hebrew University–Hadassah Medical Center is an important research center. Funds collected by Hadassah also help train young people for jobs.

Once a year, your parents probably give to the *United Jewish Appeal.* Some of the money collected by the UJA is set aside to meet the needs of Israel.

You can show your own support for Medinat Yisrael through the *Jewish National Fund.* Ever since the JNF

The trial of Alfred Dreyfus, which revealed the depth of anti-Jewish feeling in France, led Herzl to believe that Jews would never be safe without their own state in their own land.

Young Judaea, sponsored by Hadassah, is one of several Zionist youth groups in the United States. Groups like the National Federation of Temple Youth, United Synagogue Youth, and B'nei Akiva also share a love for Tzionut.

was founded in 1901, the money it has collected has been used to buy land in Israel. Some of this land was desert or swamp. The JNF has improved the land so that people can cultivate it and live on it. One important way the JNF has restored the land is by planting forests. At Tu B'Shvat you may have given money to the JNF to plant a tree in Israel. When you were born, some of your parents' friends or relatives may have sent money to the JNF for a tree to be planted in Israel in your name.

Your community may also have different Zionist youth groups, such as *Young Judaea*, which is sponsored by Hadassah. Through your religious school, you may have given toys for Israeli orphans on Ḥanukkah and Purim. This "Toys for Israeli Orphans" program is sponsored by the youth movement of the Zionist Organization of America. The programs offered by Zionist youth groups strengthen the ties that link young American Jews to Medinat Yisrael.

HAVE YOU HEARD?

You can help Zionist groups in many ways besides living in Israel. Planting trees on a happy or sad occasion is one way. Through the Jewish National Fund, more than 200 million trees have been planted in Eretz Yisrael.

REVIEW IT

1. What are two ways that members of Hadassah support Tzionut?

2. Name three Zionist groups, and discuss the one that most interests you.

רַחֲמָנוּת

RAHAMANUT
rä • hə • mä • nōōt′

Rahamanut means compassion—the feeling of sharing another creature's suffering, together with the wish to help. In a community we need a great deal of Rahamanut for other people's problems.

Rahamanut can be a kind word, a comforting touch, a mother's love.

CHAPTER EIGHTEEN

Rabbi Israel Salanter was about to eat a meal. His students watched as he washed his hands. They were surprised to see how little water he took from the full pail. They remembered how important keeping clean was to Hillel and Rabbi Akiba. So they asked him, "Rabbi, why are you using so little water? The pail is full. And if we need more water, the servant will bring another pail!"

The rabbi answered, "That servant has to fetch water from a distant well and carry the heavy pails all the way back to the house. I know it is a Mitzvah to keep clean. But my feelings of Raḥamanut tell me it is not right to carry out a Mitzvah by making other people suffer."

In this chapter you will learn that showing Raḥamanut is a way of honoring God. You will also read a story about a rabbi who kept his acts of Raḥamanut a closely guarded secret.

CHAPTER SUMMARY

Lesson 1: An act of Raḥamanut can be thought of as a kind of prayer.

Lesson 2: We show the best kind of Raḥamanut when we don't look for credit for our actions.

◄
Rabbi Moshe Leib of Sassov kept his congregation waiting on Yom Kippur eve while he comforted a crying baby.

Raḥamanut is a kind of prayer

The prophet Isaiah spoke harshly to the Jews of his day because they had failed to show Raḥamanut to widows and orphans. He told them that as long as they kept on treating others badly, God would ignore their prayers. Isaiah criticized the leaders of his time for failing to set a good example. But many Jewish leaders of later times knew that if they had to choose between praying to God and showing Raḥamanut to God's creatures, Raḥamanut came first. As you read about one such leader, ask yourself this question:

By what name do Jews call God when praying for mercy?

"AN ACT OF RAḤAMANUT IS A PRAYER, TOO"

It was Yom Kippur eve, and the time had come for saying the Kol Nidrei prayer. The congregation had gathered at the synagogue where Rabbi Moshe Leib of Sassov regularly prayed. Only the rabbi himself was absent.

The worshipers waited for Rabbi Moshe Leib as long as possible, but finally they began Kol Nidrei. Not until they had finished saying Kol Nidrei three times did the rabbi appear. The service stopped as the worried worshipers all asked what had delayed him.

"My friends," said the rabbi of Sassov, "I was on my way to the Kol Nidrei service when I heard a baby crying. I followed its cries until I came to a small house. No one answered my knocks, so I entered. I realized that the baby's parents must have left it at home while they went to the Kol Nidrei service. The baby was so sad that I could not leave it until I had rocked it back to sleep. Only then did I set out again for the synagogue."

One of the members of the congregation said, "With all due respect, rabbi, isn't prayer your first duty on Yom Kippur?"

The rabbi answered, "In our prayers, we often call God 'HaRaḥaman,' the Merciful One. An act of Raḥamanut is also a prayer."

REVIEW IT

1. Why was Rabbi Moshe Leib late for services?

2. Discuss how you would feel if your rabbi came late to your Bar or Bat Mitzvah for a similar reason.

HAVE YOU HEARD?

If you are familiar with the grace after meals—Birkat HaMazon (בִּרְכַּת הַמָּזוֹן) —you know that Jews address God as "HaRaḥa-man" (הָרַחֲמָן) during a whole section of that ceremony.

Children can show Raḥamanut for the elderly by singing songs or putting on plays in an old people's home.

Showing Raḥamanut without looking for credit

Suppose you were to show Raḥamanut by helping an elderly person cross the street. Would you rush to tell your friends and parents what a good person you were? Or would you take quiet pride in what you had done, without bragging about it to other people? Read about a rabbi who went to great lengths to keep his acts of Raḥamanut a secret between himself and God, and ask yourself:

What was special about the Raḥamanut the rabbi of Nemirov showed the poor widow?

THE CASE OF THE MISSING RABBI

The ten days that begin with Rosh HaShanah and end with Yom Kippur are especially holy. In traditional synagogues, special prayers are said before the regular morning services on each of these days. But every year, on the Friday between Rosh HaShanah and Yom Kippur, the rabbi of Nemirov would miss the special early morning services.

That the rabbi was not in the Bet Knesset, nor at a private prayer service, nor in the Bet Midrash, nor at home—this everyone knew. But no one was sure where the rabbi of Nemirov was.

The rabbi's followers insisted that the rabbi spent this Friday morning each year in heaven, pleading with God on behalf of his congregation. But one man—let's call him Mottel—doubted this. Even Moses did not go to heaven during his lifetime, Mottel argued. So Mottel decided to find out exactly where the rabbi of Nemirov went on this one Friday morning.

On Thursday night, Mottel began to put his plan into action. After evening services, Mottel hid under the rabbi's bed. There he remained all night.

In the morning, Mottel watched the rabbi's every move. To Mottel's surprise, when the rabbi went to his clothes closet, he took out a peasant's outfit. After dressing himself in the peasant's clothes, the rabbi put an ax in his belt.

When the rabbi left the house, Mottel, of course, was on his trail. He followed the rabbi into a forest, and watched the rabbi use the ax to chop up some wood. Next he followed the rabbi to a small shack on the outskirts of town.

The rabbi knocked on the door of the shack. A voice called out "Who's there?" Mottel recognized it as the voice of a poor, sick Jewish widow.

Using a peasant's voice the rabbi said, "It is Vassil, the woodcutter. I have cheap wood to sell."

Without waiting for the widow's answer, the rabbi entered the shack, with Mottel still shadowing him.

Inside the shack, the sick woman lay in rags on her

The prophet Isaiah's teachings about Raḥamanut helped shape Christian ideas of justice and mercy. This portrait of Isaiah adorns a church in Ravenna, Italy.

bed. "How can I buy even cheap wood?" she asked.

Speaking as Vassil still, the rabbi answered, "I will lend you the money. It's only six cents."

"How can I ever pay you back?" asked the woman.

"Look," said the rabbi in his peasant's voice, "a Russian peasant like me is ready to trust a poor, sick Jew like you. Can't you trust that your merciful God will help you out with six cents?"

Without waiting for a reply, the rabbi began to light a fire for her. As he did so, he started saying the special morning prayers.

Mottel never told anyone else about what he had seen of the rabbi's Raḥamanut. Instead, whenever Mottel heard someone suggest that the rabbi was in heaven on the Friday morning between Rosh HaShanah and Yom Kippur, he would say under his breath, "Actually, the rabbi may be even higher than heaven."

Mottel watched in surprise as the rabbi of Nemirov, dressed in a peasant's outfit, went into the forest and began to chop wood.

When you pet a cat, play with a dog, or nuzzle a horse, the Raḥamanut you show is as rewarding to you as to the animal that receives it.

REVIEW IT

1. List three ways in which the rabbi of Nemirov tried to keep his act of Raḥamanut a secret.

2. What did Mottel mean when he said that the rabbi of Nemirov might be "even higher than heaven"?

3. Write a story about a child who shows Raḥamanut but tries not to let other people know about it.

שָׁלוֹם

SHALOM
shä · lōm′

Shalom means "peace." It also means "hello" and "goodbye." The Hebrew word for completeness or perfection (שְׁלֵמוּת) is related to the word שָׁלוֹם.

Ever since Biblical times, a dove bearing an olive branch has been a sign of Shalom.

CHAPTER NINETEEN

Shalom may be the most important word in the Hebrew language. When we say hello and goodbye with the word "Shalom," we are wishing each other peace of mind and heart. We are also wishing for a world free from quarrels between one person and another, within families, and among nations.

This chapter explores some traditional Jewish ideas about Shalom. The first section describes the importance of peace between one person and another. In the second section, you will see how important Shalom is at home. The third section describes Jewish hopes for world peace.

CHAPTER SUMMARY

Lesson 1: Making peace between people is a Mitzvah.

Lesson 2: Sh'lom Bayit means a peaceful home.

Lesson 3: Nations will live together in peace when all accept the ideals of justice and truth.

◀

At Camp David, Maryland, Egyptian President Anwar Sadat, U.S. President Jimmy Carter, and Israeli Prime Minister Menaḥem Begin celebrate their agreement on terms for peace between Israel and Egypt—an all-too-rare example of Shalom between nations.

Shalom and personal quarrels

The rabbis taught that luxuries of all kinds cannot take the place of Shalom. "If there is no Shalom," they said, "nothing is worthwhile." They told stories that showed the importance of making peace between quarreling people.

As you read two of these stories, look for answers to these questions:

(a) *How did Aaron become known as a peacemaker?*

(b) *What legend about Elijah teaches the importance of making peace by settling arguments?*

AARON, KEEPER OF PEACE

According to the rabbis, Moses' brother Aaron was a peacemaker. Whenever any two people quarreled, Aaron would speak to each person separately. To each one he would say, "If only you knew how sorry your friend is for having quarreled with you. He takes all the blame on himself, and hopes that when you meet next you will forgive him."

By talking in this way to both quarrelers, Aaron would help them get over their anger at each other. When the two former enemies would meet next, they would beg forgiveness of one another.

One legend claims that more people mourned when Aaron died than when Moses died. Perhaps this suggests that people find it easier to love a peacemaker than a lawgiver.

Centuries after Aaron's death, Hillel urged everyone to follow Aaron's example by loving and pursuing peace.

PEACEMAKERS AND THE WORLD TO COME

One rabbi claimed he often met the prophet Elijah when he went to the marketplace.

One day, the rabbi looked around at the people in the marketplace. He said to Elijah, "Are any of these people worthy enough to have a special place in the life of the world to come?"

Elijah said that none of the people they saw around them would have a share in the world to come.

A moment later, two men appeared. They had broad smiles on their faces, and they spoke pleasantly to everyone they met.

Elijah said to the rabbi, "These two men will have a share in the world to come."

The rabbi wondered what was so special about these newcomers to the marketplace. He said to them, "Good day, my friends. I have just learned that you are very worthy men. Can you tell me why?"

HAVE YOU HEARD?

A Bet Knesset in your community may have a name that refers to Aaron's pursuit of peace. Many synagogues are called Rodef Shalom (רוֹדֵף שָׁלוֹם), or "pursuer of peace."

Elijah saw immediately from their smiling faces and peaceful ways that the two men would have a special place in the world to come.

The State of Israel has fought five major wars since 1948, but the nation also has an active peace movement. Do you recognize the black Hebrew letters on the sign displayed at this Peace Now vigil?

"We do not think of ourselves as particularly worthy," they answered, "but we do know this: whenever we see unhappy people, we try to cheer them up, and whenever we see two people quarreling, we do our best to make peace between them."

REVIEW IT

1. How did Aaron pursue peace?

2. How did Elijah teach the importance of peace?

3. Describe two things you could do to be like Aaron and the two newcomers.

Sh'lom Bayit

A good way to help spread peace throughout the world
is to start in our own homes. The Hebrew expression for
peace at home is Sh'lom Bayit, שְׁלוֹם בַּיִת. According to a
famous teacher, God Himself is interested in Sh'lom
Bayit. Read on to see what example the teacher gave, and
ask yourself:

*What did God hide from Abraham in order to create
Sh'lom Bayit?*

HOW GOD KEPT SH'LOM BAYIT
BETWEEN ABRAHAM AND SARAH

The most famous teacher of Torah is Rashi, who lived
about 900 years ago in France. When Rashi read the Torah, he found meaning in every word. He also found
meaning in what the Torah *doesn't* say.

Rashi gave as an example of God's interest in Sh'lom
Bayit the story about the three guests who visited Abraham. Abraham and Sarah prepared a meal for the guests,
who were then served outside by Abraham, while Sarah
stayed inside her husband's tent. After the meal, one of
the guests told Abraham, "I will return to you when your
wife Sarah gives birth to a son."

Sarah overheard the guest's comment through the
tent walls. Since she and Abraham were nearly 100 years
old at the time, you can understand why she laughed on
hearing what the guest promised. She said to herself,
"Now that I am like a withered leaf and my husband is
so old, am I really likely to have a child?"

Although Sarah thought her words went unheard,
God could hear them.

According to the Torah, God then asked Abraham,
"Why did Sarah laugh, saying, 'Shall I really have a child,

old as I am?' Is there anything too difficult for Me to bring about?"

Rashi studied what Sarah said to herself in the tent. He compared her original words with the words God repeated to Abraham. If you do the same thing, you will see that God did not tell Abraham that Sarah had called *him* old—only that she had called *herself* old.

According to Rashi, "When God repeated Sarah's words to Abraham, He changed them a little for the sake of Sh'lom Bayit. Abraham might have been upset at Sarah's comment that 'my husband is so old.'"

To keep Sh'lom Bayit between Abraham and Sarah, God did not tell Abraham what Sarah had said about him.

REVIEW IT

1. Give an example of how words that are missing in the Torah can tell a message.

2. Can you still call God's statement to Abraham truthful? Explain your answer.

3. Describe how you might follow God's example by not spreading gossip you heard about what someone else had done.

Shalom between nations

Every Jewish prayer service always includes prayers for peace. You probably know the song עֹשֶׂה שָׁלוֹם בִּמְרוֹמָיו , which asks God to bring peace to us and all of Israel. But Jews also look forward to a time when the entire world will live in peace.

After reading this section, you should be able to answer the following question:

According to the Jewish prophets, what are two ways in which the peaceful world of the future will differ from today's world?

"NATION SHALL NOT LIFT UP SWORD AGAINST NATION"

The prophets Isaiah and Micah looked forward to a time when there would be an end to war between nations. This time will come when all the different nations accept God's law and judgment. Once peace comes, people will turn their weapons into tools for farming.

Across from the headquarters of the United Nations in New York City stands a statue dedicated to world peace. The statue's title, "Let Us Beat Swords into Plowshares," refers to the words of Micah and Isaiah.

The prophet Zechariah also foresaw a peaceful future, in which Yerushalayim will be called the City of Truth. Many nations will come to Yerushalayim to seek God, and God will reign in truth and justice. Zechariah, speaking in God's name, said: "Speak the truth to each other, administer true and sound justice. . . . Love truth and peace."

For Jews, peace goes hand in hand with truth and justice. Rabban Simeon ben Gamaliel taught: "The world is based on three ideas: truth, justice, and peace."

SEE FOR YOURSELF

The Torah tells how God kept Sh'lom Bayit between Abraham and Sarah at Genesis 18:9–15. Prophecies of peace can be found in Isaiah 2:1–4, Micah 4:1–5, and Zechariah 8.

REVIEW IT

1. Which Hebrew prophets do people think of when they see the statue called "Let Us Beat Swords into Plowshares"?

2. What two ideas did the prophet Zechariah and Rabban Simeon ben Gamaliel connect with peace?

3. List two things that Jews your age can do to help bring about a peaceful future.

תְּפוּצוֹת

TEFUTZOT
tə • fōō • tsōt′

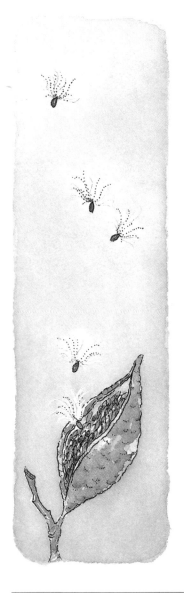

Tefutzot means Jewish settlement outside Israel. The word "Tefutzot" comes from the Hebrew word נָפַץ, meaning "to scatter." In English, "Tefutzot" is usually translated as "Diaspora."

Like the seeds of the milkweed, the seeds of Jewish life have sprouted all over the world.

CHAPTER TWENTY

The map on page 144 shows where the Jews of the world live. The larger the circle next to the name of each country, the more Jews live there. As you can see, more Jews live outside Medinat Yisrael than in it. For example, almost twice as many Jews live in North America as in Medinat Yisrael.

At times, Jews have lived in the Tefutzot because they had no other choice. For the Jews of the Soviet Union, that is still true today. They are not allowed to live fully Jewish lives in the Soviet Union, but it is not easy for them to get permission to leave. At other times, Jews have chosen to remain in the Tefutzot. That is true today for most Jews in North America. But throughout Jewish history, Jews living in the Tefutzot have had a special feeling for Eretz Yisrael.

The legend you will read in the first part of this chapter teaches that Jews can remain faithful to God in the Tefutzot. The second section describes some of the opportunities that life in the Tefutzot has given Jews.

CHAPTER SUMMARY

Lesson 1: A legend tells of God's faith that the Jews would remain true to Him while living in the Tefutzot.

Lesson 2: Many have viewed life in the Tefutzot as a chance to spread Jewish culture and to help Jews elsewhere.

Staying Jewish in the Tefutzot

No one really understands how Jews have managed to stay Jewish through centuries of life in the Tefutzot. But the old legend you are about to read shows that Jews have always had faith that they could maintain their Jewishness while living outside Eretz Yisrael. As you read the following story, ask yourself this question:

◄

For every Jew in Eretz Yisrael, about three live in the Tefutzot. Close to 6 million Jews live in the United States; about 750,000 of them are in California, where this photograph was taken.

According to the legend, how did God feel about the Jews' ability to remain good Jews in the Tefutzot?

REMAINING LOYAL JEWS IN THE TEFUTZOT

The First Temple had just been destroyed. The Babylonians had driven many Jews out of their homes in Eretz Yisrael. For the first time since they had entered the land under Joshua's leadership, more Jews would be living outside Eretz Yisrael than in it.

According to the legend, the Angels were very upset by what they saw. They said to God, "Even when the Jews lived in their own land, many of them worshiped idols instead of You. What will become of them now? Surely, living among non-Jews, more and more of them will stop worshiping You and turn to idol worship."

But God reassured the Angels. "I have great confidence in My people. Wherever they live, they will continue to worship Me. Other peoples will die out. But

HAVE YOU HEARD?

Bet HaTefutzot
(בֵּית הַתְּפוּצוֹת) —"the House of the Diaspora" —is a museum in Medinat Yisrael. It is located on the campus of the University of Tel Aviv. Exhibitions at Bet HaTefutzot give the history of most Jewish communities in the Tefutzot, including many in Eastern Europe that the Nazis destroyed. The museum also makes use of computers to help visitors find out about their family histories in different parts of the Tefutzot.

At Bet HaTefutzot, miniature displays and dioramas show the costumes and customs of Jewish communities, past and present.

even though the Jews will suffer a great deal, they will not die away. They will leave their mark on every period and in every country they live in. They will keep their faith in Me, and they will survive forever."

REVIEW IT

1. Why were the Angels afraid that Jews living in the Tefutzot would lose their Jewishness?

2. Name two events in Jewish history that seemed terrible at the time but had some good effects.

How life in the Tefutzot keeps Judaism strong

Some Jews feel that now that we have Medinat Yisrael, all Jews should move there. But many Jews feel that Jewish life in the Tefutzot is important for keeping the Jewish people strong. Try to make up your own mind as you read on, and ask yourself:

What are two ways in which life in the Tefutzot helps strengthen the Jewish people?

WORK IN THE TEFUTZOT TO STRENGTHEN THE JEWISH PEOPLE

One rabbi long ago believed that God scattered the Jewish people in the Tefutzot for the same reason a farmer scatters seeds in a field: to grow new crops. This rabbi thought God wanted Jews to live in the Tefutzot in order to encourage other people to learn about God and become Jews.

Spreading God's word does not have to mean con-

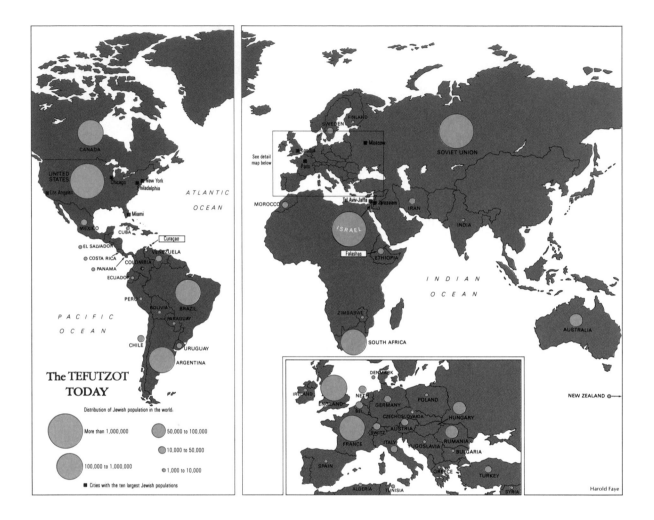

It's not always easy to know who is a Jew and who isn't, so esti-
mates of world Jewish population are far from exact. Scholars believe there are about 13 million Jews in the world, of whom 3.3
million live in Medinat Yisrael and 9.7 million in the Tefutzot. More
than three-fifths of all Jews outside Israel live in North America. Another 1.8 million Jews live in the Soviet Union and Eastern Europe,
and more than 1 million in Western Europe.

HAVE YOU HEARD?

Jewish growth in the Tefutzot has been compared to the spread of the milkweed, a plant that has grown in Eretz Yisrael since the time of the Bible. The milkweed's seeds have been scattered all over the globe, so that now the milkweed grows nearly everywhere. In the same way, life in the Tefutzot has made it possible for Jews to have a major effect on world history. The pod that contains a milkweed's seeds is called a "diaspore." This word comes from the same Greek root as "Diaspora," which is English for Tefutzot.

verting other people to Judaism. It means teaching the importance of Gemilut Ḥasadim, Derech Eretz, Kevod HaBriot, and other Jewish values you have learned about in this book. Jews living in the Tefutzot have spread these ideas and other Jewish values to the peoples of the world.

Life in the Tefutzot has also made it possible for Jews in one part of the world to come to the aid of Jews in Eretz Yisrael and elsewhere. This tradition goes back to the time of the Bible, to the story of Joseph. Joseph urged his brothers not to feel guilty about having sold him into slavery in Egypt. Joseph told them God had arranged the entire event so that years later, when there was no grain in Eretz Yisrael but a surplus in Egypt, Joseph would be able to keep his family alive.

Today, Jews in the Tefutzot continue to aid Jews elsewhere. For example, American Jews who are concerned about the problems of Jews in the Soviet Union help convince American leaders to put pressure on the Soviet government. And every year, American Jews collect millions of dollars to support different projects in Israel. Jewish leaders in the Tefutzot today work hand in hand with the leaders of Medinat Yisrael to keep the Jewish people strong.

REVIEW IT

1. What does the story of Joseph teach about the importance of Jewish life in the Tefutzot?

2. After Medinat Yisrael was founded in 1948, David Ben-Gurion criticized Zionists who remained in the Tefutzot. Imagine that you are debating this issue with him. How would you answer his criticism?

Glossary

in English alphabetical order

Adam (אָדָם), from the Hebrew word meaning "earth"; in the Torah, the name of the first human being.

Aliyah (עֲלִיָּה); literally, "going up." 1. Pilgrimage or immigration to Israel. 2. The honor of being called up to take part in the Torah reading. "Aliyah Bet" was an underground movement to smuggle Jewish refugees into Israel. See also **Olim.**

Am HaSefer (עַם הַסֵּפֶר), from the Hebrew words meaning "people" and "book"; the "people of the Book," a name originally given by the Arabs to the Jews because of the Jews' devotion to the Torah.

Bet Knesset (בֵּית כְּנֶסֶת); literally, "meeting house"; a synagogue, especially in its role as a place of prayer.

Bet Midrash (בֵּית מִדְרָשׁ); literally, "house of study"; a synagogue, especially in its role as a place for studying and teaching.

Derech Eretz (דֶּרֶךְ אֶרֶץ), from the Hebrew words meaning "path" and "land"; the right way to act.

Emet (אֱמֶת); truth, one of the most important of all Jewish values.

Eretz Yisrael (אֶרֶץ יִשְׂרָאֵל); the land of Israel, sometimes called **Zion.** See also **Medinat Yisrael.**

Gemilut Ḥasadim (גְּמִילוּת חֲסָדִים), from the Hebrew words meaning "bestow" and "loving-kindness"; the performance of kind deeds.

Kaddish (קַדִּישׁ); literally, "making holy"; a prayer said in memory of the dead.

Kevod HaBriot (כְּבוֹד הַבְּרִיּוֹת), from the Hebrew words meaning "honor" and "beings"; respect for our fellow creatures.

Kiddush (קִדּוּשׁ); literally, "holiness"; a prayer over wine on Shabbat and festivals.

Klal Yisrael (כְּלָל יִשְׂרָאֵל). 1. All Jews everywhere. 2. Jews acting together to achieve a common goal.

Knesset (כְּנֶסֶת), the parliament of **Medinat Yisrael.** See also **Bet Knesset.**

Kol Nidrei (כָּל נִדְרֵי); literally, "All Vows"; a prayer chanted at the evening service for Yom Kippur.

Medinat Yisrael (מְדִינַת יִשְׂרָאֵל); the State of Israel, founded on May 14, 1948.

Midrash: see Bet Midrash.

Minyan (מִנְיָן); literally, "a counting"; the number of people needed to hold a public prayer service; a quorum.

Mitzvah (מִצְוָה), *pl.* **Mitzvot** (מִצְוֺת); literally, "commandment." 1. Any action required by the Torah. 2. Any good deed or act of kindness.

Olim (עוֹלִים); literally, ones who "go up"; Jews who make **Aliyah** to Israel.

Pikuaḥ Nefesh (פִּקּוּחַ נֶפֶשׁ), the duty of saving a life. For Pikuaḥ Nefesh, other Mitzvot can be violated if absolutely necessary.

Raḥamanut (רַחֲמָנוּת), compassion; a feeling of sympathy, coupled with a desire to help.

Shalom (שָׁלוֹם). 1. Peace. 2. Hello. 3. Goodbye.

Sh'lom Bayit (שְׁלוֹם בַּיִת); literally, "peace at home"; good relations within the family.

Tefutzot (תְּפוּצוֹת), from the Hebrew word meaning "to scatter"; Jewish settlement outside Israel; the Diaspora.

Tzedakah (צְדָקָה), from the Hebrew word for "justice." 1. Money for the needy. 2. The act of giving charity.

Tzionut (צִיּוֹנוּת), from the Hebrew word for **Zion;** Zionism, the political movement to establish an independent state in **Eretz Yisrael.**

Yahrzeit, a Yiddish word that literally means "year time"; the anniversary of a person's death. We observe the Yahrzeit of a loved one by lighting a special Yahrzeit candle, saying **Kaddish** in synagogue, visiting the grave site, or giving **Tzedakah** in the name of the person who died.

Yerushalayim (יְרוּשָׁלַיִם); from the Hebrew words for "city of peace"; the Hebrew name for Jerusalem, a city in **Eretz Yisrael.** Ever since David made Yerushalayim the capital of his kingdom, it has been a center for Jewish hopes and prayers. Today, Yerushalayim is the capital of **Medinat Yisrael.**

Yizkor (יִזְכּוֹר); literally, "May God remember"; a memorial service said on Yom Kippur, on the last day of Passover, and at the end of Sukkot and Shavuot.

Zikaron (זִכָּרוֹן), from the Hebrew word "to remember"; memory, reminder, or memorial.

Zion (צִיּוֹן), a hill in **Yerushalayim.** In poetry, the name "Zion" often stands for the city itself or for the whole of **Eretz Yisrael.** See also **Tzionut.**

Key to pronunciation: **a** as in r**a**n, S**a**bbath; **ä** as in f**a**ther, M**a**tzah; **ā** as in p**a**y, s**e**der; **e** as in l**e**t, t**e**mple; **ē** as in dr**ea**m, H**e**brew; **ə** as in **a**bout, helpf**u**l, proph**e**t; **i** as in p**i**n, M**i**tzvah; **ī** as in f**i**ve, rabb**i**; **o** as in p**o**t, h**o**stage; **ô** as in b**ou**ght, p**o**rtion; **ō** as in b**oa**t, M**o**ses; **o͞o** as in w**oo**d, K**i**bbutz; **o͞o** as in tr**ue**, R**u**th.

INDEX